LOOKING GOOD
FEELING GOOD

FASHION AND BEAUTY IN
MID-LIFE AND BEYOND

■
NANCY TUFT

BOOKS

© 1991 Nancy Tuft
Published by Age Concern England
1268 London Road
London SW16 4ER

Editor   Claire Llewellyn
Design   Eugenie Dodd
Fashion consultant   Billie Figg
Illustrations   Jane Tyrrell
Photography   Henry Arden
Stylist   Sally Alger
Hair and make-up   Martyn Fletcher
Production   Joyce O'Shaughnessy
Copy preparation   Vinnette Marshall
Printed by Grosvenor Press Limited, Portsmouth

British Library Cataloguing in Publication Data
Tuft, Nancy
Looking good, feeling good; Fashion and beauty
in mid-life and beyond
I. Title
646.7

ISBN 0-86242-102-0

All rights reserved, no part of this work may be
reproduced in any form, by mimeograph or any other
means, without permission in writing from the publisher.

Age Concern England would like to acknowledge the
generous financial sponsorship provided by Esso UK plc
to allow this book to reach a wide audience.

Although great care has been taken in the compilation of
this book Age Concern England cannot accept responsibility
for any errors or omissions. To the best of the publisher's
knowledge, the information given in this book was correct
at the time of going to press.

Contents

Sponsor's Foreword 7

About the Author 8

Acknowledgements 9

STYLE COUNTS

Feel good, look good	11
Nobody's fashion slave	16

TAKING STOCK

First impressions	17
Check out your wardrobe	20
Check out your attitudes	23
Do your homework	24
Learn to see yourself objectively	26
Professional advisors	27
Colour analysis	30

BUDGETING AND BUYING

Spending habits	37
Clothes hunting: a serious business	39

Some guidelines on value	45
Clothes care and maintenance	49

ACHIEVING A TOTAL LOOK

Accessories — after the facts	54
Individual touches	61
Using your own creativity	63

BODY CARE

How to stay fit, active and attractive	65
Watching your weight	66
Eating: more than just food	68
Fluids are important	75
Alcohol	76
Smoking	76
Exercise	79
Personal freshness	83
Fragrance for all	84
Feet and legs	85
Hands and nails	87

Sun protection	89
Professional services	90
Body care: a final thought	95

SKIN AND FACE CARE

Female face care	98
Dental care	102
Make-up	104
Inner and outer beauty	113
Growing older gracefully	115

HAIR CARE

Day-to-day hair care	117
Protecting your hair	119
Problem solving	120
Which hairdresser?	121
Hairstyles for thinning hair	127
Hair loss	129
Wigs, toupées and hair pieces	130

SPECIAL NEEDS

After breast surgery	134
Bent backs and height losss	135
Dressing difficulties	135
Help with continence	136
Allergies	137
Skin blemishes	138
Make-up lessons for the partially-sighted	139
Overweight and housebound?	140
Hair	140

FURTHER INFORMATION

Useful addresses	143
Recommended reading	147
About Age Concern	148
Publications from ACE Books	149

Sponsor's Foreword

To mark Age Concern's Golden Jubilee, Esso felt it would be appropriate to make a contribution to the charity which would have some real lasting benefit. Ageing is something which comes to us all, and confidence plays a crucial role in the leading of an active fulfilled life, at any age. This book is written in a totally readable style, giving excellent advice in a straightforward manner — a valuable addition to any family bookshelf for easy reference.

It may seem surprising that an oil company should be the sponsors of such a publication. Esso is a wholly integrated oil company involved in the exploration for and production of oil and gas as well as the refining, distribution and marketing of its end products. As the leading national marketer in the United Kingdom, we believe in maintaining our reputation for quality service and products.

We also believe in the importance of behaving as a good neighbour and offering support to the community in which we live and work in as many ways as we can. This may range from a member of our staff acting as a local school governor to our support for national projects in the areas of education or environmental protection and includes the work of organisations such as Age Concern.

Looking Good, Feeling Good takes another step towards meeting the needs of older people by acknowledging the importance of all aspects of personal appearance in maintaining the elusive quality of self-confidence. It is one of a series of publications which Esso have been happy to be able to support.

About the Author

Nancy Tuft is an experienced author and journalist who specialises in writing for and about older people. Her highly successful guide to living abroad in retirement, *Life in the Sun,* is also published by Age Concern England. She used to work for Central Television's *Getting On* programme for older viewers and currently leads seminars on retirement planning.

Aged 58, with three adult children and five grandchildren, Nancy Tuft lives in Bromley, where she is an active member of the local University of the Third Age.

Acknowledgements

The inspiration and ideas in this book have come from a variety of sources, past and present. It has been both infinitely pleasurable and rewarding to research such a universal theme. The results were sometimes unexpected, and delightful discoveries such as Samuel Pepys' diary entry '... a silk suit which cost me much money and I pray God to make me able to pay for it', with its instantly recognisable ring, made it all the more worthwhile and deserve acknowledgement.

Research has also involved interviews and sessions with colour analysts, image consultants, hairdressers and beauty therapists; too many to thank individually by name. It has also included eavesdropping on many a conversation in Marks and Spencers as well as endless discussions with friends and contemporaries.

I am particularly grateful to journalists Billie Figg and Margaret Mason for their invaluable comments and suggestions; also to Ginny Jenkins, Clothing Adviser to the Disabled Living Foundation. Claire Llewellyn has been a helpful and supportive editor.

At Age Concern England, my thanks go to Evelyn McEwen, Enid Irving and Lee Bennett as well as to David Moncrieff for their interest, co-operation and support.

Nancy Tuft *July 1991*

Credits

We should like to express thanks for help in compiling the following pages:

- Cover pic   Pink top from a selection by EASTEX
- p19,80,81   Hints compiled by Penny Bevan Jones for *EXTEND*
- p34   Handknit cardigan from a range of kits by *ROWAN*
- p35   Leather jacket and jeans from a selection by *EMPIRE*; sweater and shoes by *HAWKSHEAD*; track pants by *NEXT*
- p70   Jodpurs from a selection by *EASTEX*; shoes from *NEXT*; earrings from *COROCRAFT*
- p71   All clothes from a selection by *NEXT*
- p72   Make-up hints taken from guidelines by Barbara Daly
- p105   Older model: Zip jacket and Chinos from a selection by *HAWKSHEAD*; shoes by *BENTLEY*
  Younger model: Check shirt and denim jacket by *HAWKSHEAD*
- p106   Older model: Chinos from a selection by *HAWKSHEAD*; shirt from *VAN GILS*; belt from *NEXT*; shoes from *BENTLEY*
  Younger model: Chinos from *EMPIRE*; shirt from *NEXT*
- p107   Suits from *JOHANNE LINDER*; shoes and belt from *NEXT*; tights from *PRETTY POLLY*; jewellery from *SAVVY*; sweater from a range of kits by *ROWAN*; black stretch velvet leggings and skirt from *NEXT*; earrings from *COROCRAFT*
- p108   Yellow suit, shirt and tie from *VAN GILS*

STYLE COUNTS

**HOW OLD WOULD YOU BE IF
YOU DIDN'T KNOW HOW OLD YOU ARE?**

Satchell Paige

■

Like it or not, today is the era of the instant visual image: clothes and appearance count. This is true for all age groups but is an especially relevant reminder for anyone over the age of 50. If you want to be taken seriously, your visual statement must be appropriately updated for the 1990s.

The old saying that you shouldn't judge a book by its cover wouldn't carry much credence with any publisher today. Shelf appeal means everything and booksellers depend on the jacket to attract the browsing customer to buy. Even well-worn classics which have stood the test of time have their jackets regularly updated. This analogy holds true for people, too. First impressions matter: they always have and they always will.

Feel good, look good

It is an interesting fact that market researchers, who stop people at random in the street, now say they can no longer rely on guess-work to estimate a person's age. This is just one indication, if one were needed, of how much physically fitter some older people are, compared with previous generations.

The mere fact that you have passed the half century mark is no excuse to abdicate all interest in personal appearance. Indeed, a whole range of new opportunities may open up as family responsibilities begin to diminish and a return to the work place is made. Women in their 50s in particular are quite likely to have more time – and money – to devote to themselves than they have had for years and many take up the challenge of updating their image with enthusiasm. Retirement, equally, can be a time of new and exciting opportunities. You may find yourself much more involved in activities outside the home than you ever were before, meeting more people, enjoying creative hobbies and taking part in sporting activities. You may be physically fitter, looking healthier and younger, and feeling good about yourself. Naturally, you will want to look good in the way you dress, as a reflection of how you feel.

Often it is trips away from home either in the UK or abroad which start you thinking about your style of dress. You see your contemporaries from other backgrounds and how they look, and then decide you are going to smarten up, or adopt a different style. It isn't always a case of imitation being the sincerest form of flattery; it may be the complete reverse. You may decide you have a lot more going for you than you had thought; perhaps you are in much better shape than many other people your age. So you make a resolution to improve and update your clothes sense. There's nothing like a challenge to polish up the old image!

The need to be positive

Older men and women need to be particularly aware of what their outward appearance seems to say about them. Society is so conditioned to see older people as 'has-beens' that dull looks and drab clothes conveniently confirm this prejudice. To counteract this stereotyped view, we need to show even more style and flair, colour and drama than before.

Why not? Our days in insurance, teaching or running our own business may be over; we may now be pensioners as well as grandparents, or even great-grandparents. However, these labels represent only one aspect of our lives, an important factor admittedly, but not the be-all and end-all of our existence. Most of us enjoy other roles too, which may be more public and less predictable. The 'grandmother' may have an exhibition of her paintings coming up soon or be preparing for a job interview or a son's wedding; the 'pensioner' may be training for the next local marathon; the 'retired grandfather' may be planning to escort a party on a tour of French cathedrals. It is important that the positive feelings generated by these various new roles should be reflected in the way we look because, rightly or wrongly, most people form their impressions of others from their outward appearance.

All this means a conscious effort on our part – but that can be fun. It will be well rewarded in terms of self-esteem and confidence, too. Even more important, the cumulative effect of an older generation which looks bright and feels surer of itself could go a long way towards defeating ageist attitudes for good.

Clothes – a confidence booster

Do you get nervous when you're invited to an unfamiliar venue? You're not alone! No one wants to appear overdressed, to look as if they'd tried too hard; on the other hand, if you turn up looking too casual, it suggests social inexperience and a lack of care.

There may be new challenges to face as you grow older: voluntary work, fundraising committees, public speaking engagements. You may be looking for a second job and going for interviews. You may be actively seeking a partner. These are all good reasons for wanting to make the most of your appearance.

Improving your dress sense and developing your own style will help you cope with most kinds of situation. You will find that wearing a jacket suggests a sense of presence and authority. Choosing up-market natural fabrics, such as silk and wool rather than polyester, gives a stamp to your style. Clothes are an investment in yourself, and it makes sense to buy the best that you can possibly afford. Wearing a blouse in a bold colour suggests confidence and imagination; one good expensive silk blouse in a positive colour is a far better buy than two or three cheaper more ordinary-looking models. Well-designed costume jewellery may be expensive, but it adds drama and presence to any outfit.

Clothes can not only boost your confidence; they can also take it away.

Never wear any colour which evokes negative feelings; if you feel dreary in grey or wishy-washy in pink, then avoid those colours. In fact, any garment which makes you feel 'down' rather than 'up' is best got rid of as quickly as possible. The best compliment anyone can ever pay you is not to admire your dress, or any one single item of clothing, but to make a spontaneous comment like, 'You're looking marvellous' or 'You do look great'. It's then that you know you've got it right!

Dress sense for men

Being well-dressed does not mean being flamboyant or standing out from the crowd. It means being appropriately and stylishly turned out for the occasion, the time, and the place. People have been clothes-conscious for centuries. 'Good clothes open all doors' was the opinion of the churchman and scholar Thomas Fuller (1608-1661), while a century later the writer Laurence Sterne (1713-1768) commented that 'a man cannot dress without his ideas get clothed at the same time'. It is interesting to note that these respectable gentlemen were referring to men's attire, not women's. One of today's most welcome trends is the resurgence of interest in clothes design for men. Older men already have the expertise necessary for occasion dressing: the knotting of ties and cravats; the wearing of a buttonhole carnation. All this is new to those generations brought up in jeans, but now wearing the more formal clothes which are enjoying a revival.

You already have a head start

Items like a Harris Tweed jacket, a tailored blazer, or a Burberry raincoat, all of which cost an arm and a leg nowadays, may be in your wardrobe already, giving you a head start over these younger men, who have to make sizeable financial commitments in order to obtain such fashion essentials. Women may own a Chanel-type cardigan suit, pleated skirt, or twin sets – all dateless classics. These can be looked at in a new light for their present-day potential (see sketches on page 15). Find new items to wear with them, or add some interesting, topical costume jewellery.

With 30 or so years of discriminating shopping experience behind you, you are probably a critical clothes shopper already. You most likely have a

◀ Update a favourite classic fitted jacket with soft culottes for a newer, more flattering line.

▼ The short top of a standard cardigan suit looks neat and imaginative above a flowing skirt.

greater understanding and knowledge than your children of fabrics, as well as an ability to judge the quality of a garment by its lining and finish – hems, buttonholes and so on. Standards have certainly deteriorated, but at least you have some basis for comparison, and this is a distinct advantage, whether you are shopping for new or second-hand bargains.

Nobody's fashion slave

Some people are not enamoured with the concept of fashion. George Bernard Shaw referred to fashions as being induced epidemics whilst Queen Marie of Romania observed that fashion existed for women with no taste. A more contemporary comment from Yves St Laurent is that while fashions fade, style is eternal. Jean Muir agrees: 'To be in fashion is to be out of style.'

But whose style is more important? Yours or the designers'? As an older shopper, you are unlikely to be unduly impressed by the snob-value of designer labels. You probably like to judge a garment on its own merits. You may have seen various expressions of style before, how the cycles come and go, so you will be well equipped to ignore the fads but, hopefully, sufficiently perceptive to recognise important trends.

The direction of the 1990s is towards more 'grown-up' clothes of better quality and design. Style has been subservient to fashion for too long; there has been too much poorly made ephemera in High Street shops which has no appeal whatsoever for the mature customer. In today's adverse economic climate, clothes are tending to revert to being conservative and traditional. Yet, within that framework there is ample space for personal choice and individuality. The clothes climate is at last beginning to look promising.

TAKING STOCK

I THINK SOMEHOW WE LEARN WHO WE REALLY ARE AND THEN LIVE WITH THAT DECISION

Eleanor Roosevelt

■

Taking stock is about taking charge of your own appearance. It's a matter of working out a compromise: accepting the inevitable and setting achievable goals. The decision is yours. How smart and attractive can you reasonably expect to be?

You need to accept that looking after your appearance in later life may absorb more time and effort than it ever did in the past. This is a sign of the times; people of all ages are infinitely more conscious of self-presentation than ever before. You will have to work extra hard on developing a self-critical faculty – an ability to see your outward appearance objectively – and learn what suits you as an individual. Without this ability it's all too easy to play safe and shy away from new challenges.

Whatever your preferred style, the degree of enthusiasm, energy and effort you put into achieving your goal will certainly be reflected in the end result.

First impressions

Your top-to-toe image is what any stranger sees for the first time. Rightly or wrongly this initial encounter will influence other people's ideas about you. The instant picture is composed of:

the clothes you wear
the way you wear your clothes
your grooming.

The clothes you wear

Clothes are a means of self-expression and self-enhancement which is accessible to everyone, regardless of age or sex. Art historian James Laver described clothes as 'the furniture of the mind made visible'.

Sadly, many older people tend to feel that their appearance just isn't worth thinking about: there are too many other things to do with their time. This is a pity because it is a wasted opportunity. Only a genius or absolute eccentric can get away with such casual disregard for the outward image. When people wear clothes that are ugly and outdated, it is often assumed that their ideas and attitudes are stuck in the same time warp. This may well be a false notion, but the unspoken message is powerful and off-putting. It suggests someone who is neither interested nor involved in the world of today.

Most people find shopping for clothes a frustrating and wearisome business. Complaints about cramped cubicles, loud music, unhelpful assistants, and nothing available in your size are all quite legitimate, but shared by many people of all ages. Excuses such as these shouldn't be used by the reluctant shopper as reasons for being negative. Don't let these petty annoyances obscure your goal, which is to look your best – not only for yourself, but for those around you.

The way you wear your clothes

Well-chosen clothes deserve to be shown off properly by someone who stands tall, sits upright and moves confidently and easily.

Check your posture so that walking and standing well become second nature.

Take frequent exercise to keep body and joints flexible and mobile. Choose an activity you enjoy, such as golf, swimming, dancing or walking.

Sit, don't slump, when watching TV.

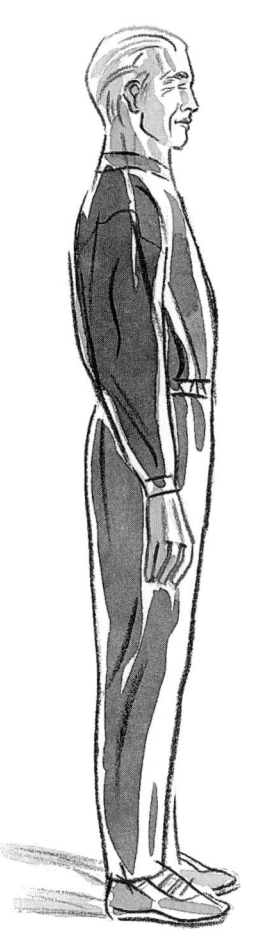
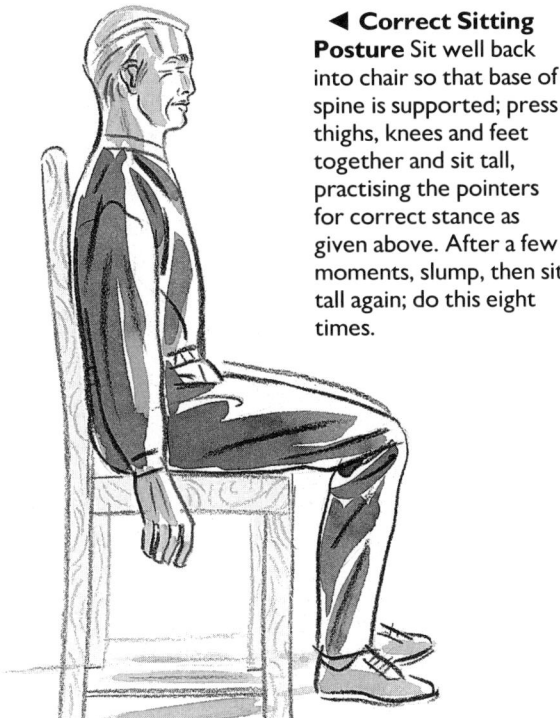

◀ **Correct Standing Posture** Weight forwards, towards toes, knees gently contracted and centred over the middle of the feet, hips straight above the knees. With seat pulled under, hold lower abdomen as flat as possible: lower the shoulders. Stretch the neck at the back, keeping chin in and the crown of head pointing to ceiling – like a puppet on a string.

◀ **Correct Sitting Posture** Sit well back into chair so that base of spine is supported; press thighs, knees and feet together and sit tall, practising the pointers for correct stance as given above. After a few moments, slump, then sit tall again; do this eight times.

Your grooming

Grooming covers the head-to-toe details of hair, feet, hands and fingernails, skin and teeth, all of which should look well cared for. Good grooming is an indication of self-worth – of how much we like ourselves. This isn't unduly narcissistic. If you don't appear to value yourself and your appearance, how can you expect a favourable response from others?

Grooming is an important social activity in the lives of animals. When an animal stops grooming itself, allowing its fur or feathers to become ragged and ill kempt, it is usually an early indication of ill-health. The same might be said of humans. Never underestimate the positive role played by grooming in people's lives. It can be a valuable antidote to stress, worry and depression.

There are times, of course, when people lose interest in their appearance, perhaps due to illness or bereavement. It's always good news when people begin to take an interest in their appearance once again after a sad or lonely episode in their lives. Often the turning-point can be encouraged by a relative, neighbour or friend suggesting some appearance-related activity. It may be nothing more momentous than a visit to the hairdresser, a facial, a sauna or a massage, but it can act as a welcome back to the living world.

Much grooming takes place outside the home, at hairdressers and beauty salons, which are now classless and ageless in their clientele. As well as benefitting from the professional skills available, the client can also enjoy the feeling of being pampered and looked after. What used to be seen as an indulgence for the rich is now regarded as routine body maintenance, and a means to well-being for all.

Unisex hairdressers are now well established. Men can also enjoy saunas, Turkish baths and massage at health farms and hydros. Local fitness and leisure centres, and even some beauty salons, are now offering face and body treatments for male customers.

Check out your wardrobe

How would you describe your wardrobe: as an instantly wearable collection, or a storehouse from the past? Does your wardrobe consist of a well-organised assembly of interesting, varied and coordinated outfits which are suitable for putting on today? This needn't imply that everything is a recent purchase. You may well have owned several garments for some years. Many basic classics are ageless but they need reviewing regularly in a contemporary light and putting together with updated accessories.

On the other hand, does your present wardrobe contain too many leftovers from a life you used to lead? Typical items are any of the following: a dinner suit or ball gown which will never fit you again; jodhpurs or other riding gear which you have long outgrown; a hot, heavy overcoat which is too warm for the car; for women – anything in a size 12 when you are now size 16; numerous pairs of boots and shoes of all shapes and sizes, none of which is remotely comfortable today. Maybe you did pay a lot for these garments at the time; maybe there is still a lot of wear left in them, but are you ever going to wear them again? The acid test of whether you are living in the present depends on honest answers to these questions.

Are your clothes appropriate to your current lifestyle?

Are they the right size for your body shape *now?*

When people have recently retired, it often happens that there is an imbalance in their wardrobe – too many office suits and not enough leisurewear. It may take a while before you establish what your new lifestyle will be, so allow for a transitional period before taking the navy pinstripe to Oxfam, and don't rely too heavily on a beige anorak in the meantime.

▶ Pleated skirts are comfy, stylish and out of the ordinary under straight-hanging loose sweaters: try the men's classic crew neck over a tie-neck blouse.

Helpful advice for hoarders

However strong you may be on sentiment, most people are short of storage space. Give top priority to your current clothes collection; garments need to have air and space around them, and you need to be able to see at a glance what is available.

Hoarders tend to have the kind of wardrobe where every garment is packed in so tightly that it's impossible to drag anything out without a struggle. Hangers get twisted and caught up; garments get snagged, pulled about and creased. If you really can't bear to let anything go, at least separate one season's outfits from another's and store them apart.

If you have garments which you never wear, why hold on to them? They may be someone else's bargain. Check on their current worth before deciding to sell or give them away. The following are all possible outlets:

- second-hand sale, via a classified ad, car boot sale, wardrobe dealer or nearly-new shop
- charity shop
- jumble sale
- local amateur dramatic society
- dressing-up box for grandchildren or local playgroup.

A wardrobe full of clothes and nothing to wear?

The predicament of having an uneven mixture of mismatched separates, none of which quite works with anything else, is common to all ages. The retired person, however, has less incentive to remedy the situation than someone who has to face the office each day.

A wardrobe with unfilled gaps may indicate one of two things: that you are a reluctant shopper who needs to improve on staying power and the organisation to plan whole outfits; or, that you are a compulsive shopper who grabs anything and everything that takes your fancy. Random buying, unless you are very sure of what suits you and the rest of your wardrobe, is seldom successful.

Most people have too many clothes – there are after all only seven days in a week. Some judicious pruning and weeding out may be called for, just to let some daylight in. Then you may be able to see where the gaps really are.

Professional advice on wardrobe planning is readily available. Such advice will undoubtedly help you become a more selective shopper (see p 27).

Check out your attitudes

Sometimes it is your perceptions rather than your clothes which need a good shake-up. Ageism isn't only in the eye of the beholder. How do you see yourself?

Mutton or lamb?

The moth-eaten old saying 'mutton dressed as lamb' keeps many older women from maximising their looks and keeping their appearance up to date. In their eyes, any new type of garment or hairstyle tends to be labelled 'young' and is, therefore, taboo. Of course, there are a few garments best left to younger wearers – the mini or microskirt is an obvious example – but there are not many others. The ability to wear a certain style is more likely to be determined by body shape than by age.

The insidious effect of this play-safe attitude is that many women censor clothes which are eminently suited to their lifestyle (see photographs on page 70). Many women shun culottes, for example; yet they are casual and versatile, and look far more dressy and feminine than trousers.

Older men may be equally cautious and unadventurous when it comes to new styles, even when the practical advantages are obvious; 'chinos' and elasticated or drawstring cotton trousers are examples of ageless casual summer wear with good washability (see photograph on page 106). Why ignore them?

Where clothes are concerned, of course, there are actually very few garments that are totally new. Most of them are constantly recycled, appearing and reappearing over subsequent generations. Camisoles and camiknickers are currently enjoying a revival. Other garments may be given a new name; culottes used to be known as a divided skirt, and then gauchos – they are all the same garment.

Enjoy comfort with style

Clothes which are comfortable rightly occupy a high priority, but comfortable clothes don't have to be shapeless and shabby, in boring drab colours. Comfort and style can and do go hand in hand (see photograph on page 70). Think of cotton sweatshirt leisurewear for men as well as women; skirts, trousers, or jogging pants have elasticated waists which make for easy movement in keep-fit classes, the garden or out walking. Tops come in a variety of styles and the choice of colours – bright, dark and pastel – is endless.

Do your homework

When young people go shopping for clothes, many of them know what they are looking for. They have a clear picture of the look they want to achieve and how to put it all together. Their eyes are trained to absorb the top-to-toe picture of clothes and accessories which are displayed in the boutiques and chain stores where they habitually shop.

Older browsers who enjoy looking round the shops on a regular basis have probably picked up much of this visual awareness, but if you're the kind of person who doesn't enjoy shopping, and only shop when you have to, you may have some catching up to do. The old army adage 'time spent on reconnaissance is seldom wasted' applies equally to clothes shopping! Fortunately, a lot of background know-how can be acquired at home via television or the printed word.

Television

The Clothes Show on BBC1 is regular viewing for millions of people of all ages. The production team actively seeks out interesting fashion news items from all over the country. The result is a range of informative features on all aspects of the design and production of clothes and accessories.

The programme takes the elitism out of fashion and looks at it critically as a service industry catering for consumers in Manchester, Leeds, Glasgow and so on. It certainly isn't just a young programme – older viewers will find plenty to interest them. Regular competitions encourage viewer participation, especially the annual knitting competition.

There is a monthly *Clothes Show* magazine on sale in newsagents, as well as an annual exhibition.

Magazines and newspapers

It's useful to keep in touch with the ever-changing magazine market and this you can easily do by having a browse in your local newsagents. Take every opportunity to look through the expensive glossies such as *Vogue* and *Cosmopolitan* because this helps develop visual awareness. The weekly colour supplements also carry fashion features and bear witness to the growing interest in style for men.

Your instant reaction to such style features may be 'But who on earth can afford clothes at those silly prices?' Don't be too literal concerning the small print. Observe and absorb the look. What the fashion writer is illustrating and interpreting is an underlying trend which will soon filter down the fashion chain and be available at prices most people can afford.

Retirement magazines such as *Choice* and *Saga* publish fashion features for the over-50s and carry special offers. However, if you restrict yourself to looking at and buying what is generally perceived as 'suitable' and 'acceptable' for the older person, you find yourself following a rather conformist line and missing out on new ideas.

Family magazines covering a wide age range, such as *Family Circle* and *Living*, are sold in supermarkets. *Family Circle* includes consumer-based articles featuring stockists of interesting clothes for women of size 16 and over. If hard-to-get sizes are your specific problem, then this kind of information needs cutting out and keeping in your own style folder. Articles which include new information about stockists are also worth cutting out and keeping for future reference.

Learn to see yourself objectively

Use your mirror

A full-length mirror (and preferably a free-standing one for a back view) is an absolute necessity at home. You should be using it constantly.

You may have owned a particular garment for years and feel you know how it looks on you, but it will appear slightly different each time you wear it with other separates and accessories. The proportions may change and so the overall effect is going to be different. The best and easiest way to develop a critical eye is by always trying on more than one outfit and comparing results. This applies to trying on garments in a shop as well as at home. What you are subjecting yourself to is a critical assessment of the way clothes look on you.

Once you have succeeded in putting together a pleasing combination of clothes and accessories, it's a good idea to write down its composition, rather than trust your memory. Take care to include every last detail. See 'Achieving a Total Look' (p 54) for further advice.

Using the video

A few up-market stores have been developing a video service enabling customers to see themselves in the new outfit on video, before committing themselves to an expensive purchase. Anyone with a video camera of their own might be able to adapt this idea for home use, say at the beginning of a season when you're re-appraising your wardrobe. The image given on an all-round video is a far more realistic assessment than the one reflected in static mirrors.

Use the young

Daughters often show an active interest in their mother's appearance; they provide positive encouragement, and comments are invariably constructive, even if critical on occasion (see photographs on page 107).

A daughter can be a valued shopping companion, introducing you to certain hair salons or other places where you wouldn't normally go. She may also provide a convenient home-based opportunity to try on, compare and assess garments in new or much younger styles (see photographs on page 107). Even if you and your daughter are not quite the same size, you can get an idea of the general effect in front of a mirror. Do take advantage of this opportunity to try on glitzy earrings, hair ornaments and the like.

Men, too, can take advantage of the occasional item in a son's wardrobe (see photograph on page 106). A garment like a leather jacket may be new for you; it's far less inhibiting to slip this on and get the feel of it in front of a mirror at home than to try it on furtively in public under the idle gaze of a shop assistant. Once you are reassured that something does suit you, you can then seek it out in the shops with more confidence.

The advantages of benefitting from young experience needn't be dependent on having a family living conveniently nearby. Cultivate younger relatives and friends and use them as a source of advice. They will be flattered to be consulted and you will receive valuable feedback from a generation weaned on fashion and who are only too ready to share their know-how (see photographs on page 105).

A word of warning. Don't get into the habit of relying too much on others for second opinions. You must learn to trust your own judgement. Clothes have got to feel right on you as well as look right. Only you can be the ultimate judge of that, however pressing the advice you receive.

Professional advisors

There are a number of commercial organisations involved in colour analysis, style and image guidance. Names to look out for include Academy of Colour and Style, Colour Me Beautiful, Colourflair, First Impressions, House of Colour and Your True Colours (see pp 143–146). Each organisation has a countrywide network of consultants or counsellors, most of whom operate under a franchise or licensing arrangement but are company trained. These consultants hold individual and group sessions, for men as well as women. They also take part in demonstrations and give talks to groups.

Unless you live in a remote rural area, there shouldn't be much difficulty in finding professional advice. Try looking in the *Yellow Pages*; alternatively phone or write to the head office for a local contact (see pp 143-146).

Colour analysis fees vary; those for style and wardrobe guidance are usually slightly more, but will depend on the length of the session. Men are often offered a combined package, including both colour and image.

As an older person, you will want to feel that the advice you are paying for is sufficiently individual and appropriate for your lifestyle. By way of introduction, you may like to go to the library for some background reading first. Titles from Colour Me Beautiful include *Colour for Men, Always in Style* and *The Complete Style Guide from Colour Me Beautiful*. Further details are on page 147. While books are no real substitute for actual colour analysis, you can learn a lot about proportion and how to diagnose your own body shape from *The Colour and Style File* by Sheffield-born Barbara Jacques, founder of the Academy of Colour and Style. All the above books are published by Piatkus.

The following information may help you decide whether or not either or both kinds of professional advice will be helpful for you.

Wardrobe, style and image guidance

Your consultation may be on a one-to-one basis, or via a workshop with three or four other clients, which gives people the opportunity to learn from each other. A style session reinforces the fact that dressing well means wearing clothes that fit and hang well, along with the right choice of accessories. You will be given a style file, folder or booklet at the end to take home as a reminder.

Your style consultant will advise on body shape and proportion; she will offer recommendations on how to disguise figure faults, along with compensatory tips for the tall and the short, the overweight and the skinny. Jacket shapes can make a considerable difference to the way a person looks; so can dress designs; so can details like lapels and pockets.

'Personal packaging' encompasses more than clothes, however. Self-presentation includes all the elements which form part of our appearance: hair, spectacles, shoes, skin, even eyebrows. Men are often advised to pluck their eyebrows, especially if they are bushy and meet in the middle, making the face look unnecessarily angry or fierce.

Professional advice often includes the self-evident, like the importance of the right tie and socks to create a good impression, or the necessity – if you have belt loops – to wear a belt! Sometimes the advice is less immediately obvious. For example, women are advised not to wear dangly earrings at meetings or other occasions when they want to be listened to; earrings which move can distract attention.

Since many large, well-known companies are hiring image consultants to run courses for their staff, there is sometimes an over-emphasis on so-called power dressing, which is seen as a way of getting on in business. Image consultancy clients have included a rush of MPs (anxious about the televising of Parliament), a whole generation of young men wearing suits for the first time, younger women and married women returners – all competing at executive level.

There are many situations in later life when you won't get a second chance to make a good impression and can benefit from a confidence booster.

- You may have just relinquished full-time family responsibilities or have retired early, and are job hunting and seeking interviews.
- Your career may be blossoming and you are seeking promotion.
- You may feel you've let yourself go and want to smarten up, yet aren't sure where or how to begin.
- You may be faced with a new opportunity or challenge, serving as a committee member, speaking in public and so on.
- You may be making a positive effort to extend your social life by getting out and about more, and meeting new people.

Colour analysis

Colour analysis advises how accepted colour theory relates to the way we look and the clothes we wear. Anyone who has been to painting classes will already know that colours, as well as skin pigments, are either predominantly blue-based or yellow-based.

In a colour analysis session, the client sits in a chair in front of a mirror, without make-up, shoulders swathed in a colourless sheet. The consultant then demonstrates the effect against the face of varying swatches or drapes of differing shades and tones from a wide spectrum of colours. The results are usually obvious, even to an absolute beginner.

Wearing a mismatched type of colour for your skin tone can make you look tired, washed-out, boring or years older than you are. Wearing an appropriate shade which complements your natural colouring will greatly enhance your whole appearance.

Whichever system of colour analysis is used, and there are many, clients come away with a wallet-sized collection of colour swatches which they can take with them when they shop. For women, there is usually a make-up demonstration using company products in complementary colours.

The method of colour analysis most popularly employed by the American-based companies, which pioneered colour analysis in the UK, uses a four-way or four-seasons approach. This is demonstrated by a colour wheel divided into four segments. The fact that these four divisions of colour are named after the seasons is not in itself significant but does make them easier to remember.

People with predominantly yellow skin tones are put in either one of two of the sections, called Autumn or Spring, and they need warm golden-toned colours. People with blue undertones in their skin are categorised as Winter or Summer, both of whom suit cool, blue-based colours.

Other companies have developed different systems incorporating wider aspects of colour theory besides cool and warm. For example, Your True Colours (see p 146) emphasises the importance of matching for tonal qualities: bright or muted; light, dark or medium. Clients' swatches are made up for them on an individual basis. The clients of Colourflair (see p 144) get a personal colour fan with sufficient flexibility to allow for individual variations in skin tone.

There are numerous plus points about colour analysis.

You are shown a wide range of colours which complement your natural colouring. You will look healthier and more attractive as a result of wearing these colours.

Your clothes will be flattering and show you at your best.

You will learn how to put colours together in an interesting way.

When shopping, you will know what to avoid and thereby save expensive failures.

You will be able to plan your clothes budget better.

You will find packing a holiday wardrobe much easier.

If you wear make-up, you will be sure this matches the colours you use.

Colour analysis for men

Older men, who have traditionally hidden behind the office uniform of a dark suit, conventional shirt and restrained tie, have not had the same opportunity as women to develop their colour and dress sense. Men tend not to be so familiar with the colours which suit them or as used to selecting colours and garments to create an integrated look (see photographs on p 108).

A retirement wardrobe is likely to put an increased emphasis on the casual and informal look, but it still needs careful planning if it is going to work. A versatile collection of casual trousers, separate jackets – formal and informal – shirts and coloured sweaters, needs thoughtful assembly. An important part of colour analysis is learning how to put colours together. Holiday and leisure clothes nowadays are extremely bright and colourful. Too much choice can lead to mistakes. By learning which are the right colours for you, you can be sure of making the most of your appearance.

When you have a choice

If you live in a town and seek advice on colour analysis, you will probably have a choice of representatives from more than one company. How do you pick the one which best suits your needs? Approaches to the subject of colour analysis vary, and companies are still developing their methods in what is becoming a growing and competitive market.

The best recommendation is word-of-mouth from a contemporary whose appearance you admire and who can tell you first-hand whether they found the experience good value for money. There is now a national City and Guilds qualification which has evolved in conjunction with the UK Federation of Image Consultants. Their shared aim is to maintain high standards. Subject areas covered by this examination include colour analysis, make-up, male analysis, style and image, presentations to corporations and talks to clubs and groups. Obviously it will take time for students to work through the new course and start practising as qualified consultants.

If you have no personal recommendation to rely on, read and compare the respective leaflets you are offered, bearing in mind that these are standard publicity material issued by the parent company. Whichever company's consultant you choose, much of her guidance will depend on her manner – her personal and communicative skills. You can usually get an impression of her personality over the telephone; don't hesitate to ask questions in order to discover how well she empathises with your age group.

Some consultants are themselves in the over-50s age range, which usually reassures audiences at presentations and introductory demonstrations to groups such as the Women's Institutes, Townswomen's Guilds or retirement groups. Such presentations are ideal publicity for consultants and are all part of their job. You might like to suggest an introductory talk on colour analysis and style for the forthcoming programme of your own club.

◀▼A strong jacket – defined in line and bold colour – imparts poise to the wearer and conveys a sense of confidence that helps you cope with most situations. Look for clean hang, well defined details, adequate length, positive colour.

▼ To leap from basic to creative knitting is fulfilling - and fashionwise too. This stunning cardigan designed by Kaffe Fassett can be made from a kit containing patterns and yarns.

◀ Track trousers help you look and feel active. In neutral shades, they team with a great variety of tops.

▼ A leather jacket gives the wearer a buoyant image that flatters an older man without suggesting he is trying too hard.

▼ A colour-toned camisole will often turn an old print skirt and a shirt into a team.

◀ Unrelated jumpers and trousers come together if colour-linked by a polo sweater toned to trousers.

▼ A classic waist-covering cardigan – consider the men's ranges – can streamline random trousers and shirts into outfits.

BUDGETING & BUYING

NOTHING IS CHEAP WHICH IS SUPERFLUOUS, FOR WHAT ONE DOES NOT NEED IS DEAR AT A PENNY

Plutarch

∎

Spending habits

Recent consumer reports on spending by older people reveal that this age group spends only slightly less on clothes and personal appearance products than the rest of the adult population. In addition, there is a top ten per cent of the group who are big spenders, with a clothes budget well exceeding the national average.

Signal International, one of the marketing organisations monitoring these spending habits, called their report *Over 55s – The Invisible Consumers*. Why are these consumers invisible? Why aren't the fashion, beauty, hairdressing and related industries catering more for older shoppers? The top ten per cent are only the tip of the iceberg. What about the huge submerged sector, who need a little more wooing and winning, coaxing and persuading before they part with their hard-earned wealth?

The disappearing younger market

The most significant factor for the fashion and hairdressing world in the 1990s is not just that the population now includes a bigger proportion of affluent older shoppers than ever before, but that this is combined with a lower proportion of young people. Falling school rolls and fewer teenagers must mean a shift from the diminishing teens and 20s market. It is now the over-50s who are firmly in the ascendant. Yet, who would ever suspect this from the message put out by advertising and promotion, or from the High Street window displays?

Uninspired older shoppers

Statistics may be interesting but individual spending habits are powerful. Of course, stylish dressers don't suddenly cease to be clothes-conscious at a particular age. They still possess sufficient verve and energy to seek out the goods and services which match up to their expectations. But what about the rest – Mr and Mrs Average? They have a tendency to play safe, to be well-groomed, neat and tidy but that's as far as sartorial ambition goes. The situation isn't helped by manufacturers and retailers who have ignored older shoppers in favour of the young market. This neglect of mature customers has bred negative attitudes. Passive consumers with low expectations tend to take the easy way out. They avoid shopping for clothes, relying exclusively on their local chain store, a non-challenging, impersonal outlet offering self-selection.

Stores like this are the perfect place for everyday value-for-money 'topping-up' items, but habitual reliance on such safe browsing pastures will inevitably encourage sheep-like tendencies. Anyone who wants to look a little different from the rest of the herd may well have to try a lot harder. It takes a positive effort to achieve a more creative look – one which tells the world you are a vital and interesting personality, someone worth knowing in fact!

Balancing your budget

Are you allocating a reasonable proportion of your time and income to your appearance? British people on the whole tend to put a much lower budget priority on appearance than other Europeans or Americans. It shows in the way we look. We are neither the best-dressed nation in the world, nor are we the healthiest (see Body Care p 65).

Only you can decide what you can afford to spend on your appearance in the light of your income and outgoings. However, do bear in mind that how you look is going to affect how you feel, every day.

Whatever your budget, it may be worth checking that it is distributed in a way that maximises your total appearance. Do you perhaps focus too much on clothes? A typical British trend is to go for quantity rather than quality, and to ignore the value of accessories. Are your hair and face getting a fair share of the available resources? More attention to hair, updated make-up lessons and a fitness course, can make a big improvement to your overall look.

Equally important are regular visits to the dentist, (even denture wearers need to check on fit); to the optician to review glasses; to the chiropodist for foot care. Are you neglecting these forms of maintenance merely because these services which used to be free now have to be paid for?

Clothes hunting: a serious business

Clothes hunting is not just serious, it's an adventure. You need to be clear about your objectives. What are you aiming for? What are you trying to achieve?

- You are consciously creating your own style, based on clothes which are compatible with your body shape and reflect your individual taste. You are not just copying the look of the moment.
- Your search may cover a wide variety of different sources. Sometimes you will be going up-market for a sound investment, such as a jacket or coat. At other times you may snap up something cheap and cheerful, when and wherever you come across it.
- Don't limit yourself by sticking to shops in the same price band. Be open-minded and adventurous. Interesting clothes and accessories can come from a variety of sources, and include good-as-new bargains from dress agencies, charity shops and jumble sales.
- Your hunting grounds are boundless and not restricted to your home area. Take advantage of out-of-town visits, weekend breaks and holidays abroad to seek out interesting additions to your wardrobe.

A designer-dressmaker on the doorstep?

The recent growth in small businesses has encouraged some former fashion students to start up on their own as designer-dressmakers in their own locality. Often they specialise in bridal wear for which there is a strong seasonal demand, but not necessarily or exclusively so. They may advertise in the local press, *Yellow Pages* or *Thomson Directory*, but more often than not, business grows by personal recommendation.

Take advantage of opportunities like this, following up recommendations when they arise. You can always request to see samples of finished garments.

Shopping awaydays

No longer is London the great fashion mecca. Clothes of high quality and considerable style can be found in every region of the country. *Archer's Good Clothes Guide,* an annual publication, (see p 147) is compiled in the manner of a good restaurant guide and gives details of the best boutiques throughout the country for women's clothes, accessories and jewellery. When can we look forward to men's clothes being added? Like restaurants, some of the most interesting shops tend to be found in clusters around a particular area, making a visit a tempting proposition, especially since many of the locations are attractive places in their own right.

Visiting a factory shop provides an interesting shopping outing as well as the opportunity to buy seconds or lengths of fabric. Since factories tend to be located off the beaten track, you will probably need your own transport. Those without cars might consider arranging a group or club outing in a hired minibus. A series of regional guides to factory shops gives opening times, map and parking details: some editions are available from W H Smith. In case of difficulty, they are obtainable direct by mail order from the compiler, Gillian Cutress (see the address on p 147.)

Keep an open mind

When hunting for new clothes, be wary of making dismissive judgements about shops or labels based on past impressions. These may be long out of date. A number of retail chains and fashion houses have been around for a long time. They are familiar names to older shoppers, but what these names stood for years ago may no longer be valid. Their merchandise has to be judged by the standards of today's market place.

C&A, with well over 100 stores throughout the UK, is an example of a popular chain well-known for its competitively priced clothes. What may be less well-known is that its range of ski-wear is ahead of those in other chain stores and that it is now including more up-market collections in some of its city-based stores.

Many British companies have had a 1990s revamp of their old image, either by using new designers or by their marketing. One example is Windsmoor, a firm anxious to shed the frumpy image it felt it had acquired. This is an example of a British fashion house growing up and becoming aware of the increasing competition from Europe, where older dressing does not mean being fuddy-duddy.

Problem solving

Having a body which is anything other than average in size and proportion can impose limitations on your range of choice. This does not mean you are a freak, and should not encourage indulgent feelings of pessimism and despair. The real problem is the lack of flexibility in sizing. Only by informing manufacturers and retailers of your shopping difficulties will anything ever be done. Remember you probably represent hundreds of other disappointed shoppers across all age groups.

Possible solutions may be found by writing to the service pages of a wide variety of magazines. They may have useful up-to-date information about firms which cater for particular sizes, or about reasonably priced made-to-measure clothes.

Do be creative about any 'problems' you may have. You may be able to tackle them in unexpected ways. For example, a big tummy is not unusual in older women, but can make clothes-buying difficult. If this is a problem, you could take a look at shops and departments which specialise in maternity clothes. Gone are the shapeless maternity garments of yesterday. The fact that so many women now carry on working well into their pregnancy means there are some very smart outfits available, as well as more casual trousers with matching tops. Equally, ordinary shops provide a range of elastic-waisted, unwaisted or drop waisted dresses which could prove suitable.

Special sizes: a guide to the High Street

An increasingly large number of familiar High Street names are catering for customers requiring merchandise in special sizes.

Women: 5'3" and under

C&A	Petite sizes 10–18 in 19 branches
Debenhams	Anne Brooks label, sizes 8–16, in 76 stores
Eastex	Sizes 10–20, in most department stores
Jaeger	Cameo Collection, sizes 6–14, in 70 outlets
John Lewis	Petite range, sizes 8–16, in 16 branches
Marks & Spencer	Petite range, sizes 7–13, in 60 branches
Richard Stump	Sizes 10–20, in John Lewis and House of Fraser stores
Windsmoor	Précis Collections, sizes 8–16, in department stores

Tall women

Long Tall Sally	Sizes 12–20 for 5'8"-6'2". Ten shops plus mail order from the address on page 146
Marks & Spencer	Long fittings, in most stores
Wallis	Sizes 8–14 in 34" skirt length, in most stores

Women: size 16+

BHS	Collection Plus, sizes 18–24, in 90 branches
C&A	Renoir range, sizes 16–26, in 40 branches
Debenhams	Emma Daniels range, sizes 14–26, in 38 branches
Evans	Sizes 14–30 in 245 branches, some of which are in department stores

John Lewis	Sizes 18–24, in 15 branches
Marks & Spencer	Fashions for the fuller figure sizes 18–24, in 30 branches

Men: big and/or tall

High & Mighty	28 shops as well as mail order catalogue from the address on page 145.

Shopping by post

Mail order shopping from catalogues has obvious advantages if you live a long way from shops or don't feel up to a lot of footslogging. It can save a lot of time, and may offer additional choices in large and small sizes. However, not everyone wants to be weighed down with a hefty volume containing not only clothes, but assorted household items, as well as all the accompanying paperwork involved in buying on credit. The emphasis often seems to be on selling credit rather than selling clothes, the quality of which can be variable.

There are many reliable small specialist firms selling high-quality merchandise direct to the customer by means of a brochure. The advantage of direct selling is that the considerable shop mark-up is avoided, yet the consistency of high quality can be maintained. Typical examples are Patra Selections, who make silk blouses, dresses and underwear, and Acorn Designs who make jackets, waistcoats and cloaks in Austrian loden, a hardwearing and warm wool fabric. One of Gillies, an individual designer firm in Glamorgan, uses unusual and interesting fabrics to make garments which would cost more if bought in the shops. Both firms send sketches of their seasonal collections for women – day, evening and holiday wear – together with sample fabric swatches. Small firms like these, the addresses of which are on pages 143-146, welcome feedback and suggestions from their appreciative and loyal customers.

Some of the disadvantages of mail order – the uncertainty of when a home delivery is going to be made, and the return of garments which don't fit or suit – are avoided by a recent development in the High Street, Next Directory Stores. There are now over 50 of these shops in High Streets throughout the UK. They display garments from the Next Directory, a mail order catalogue containing fashion for men, women and children. These garments are available in the stores for trying on and purchasing on the spot. Any item in the catalogue which you wish to try can usually be delivered to the store within 24 hours or – for a fee – to the customer's home. Clearly, however, this method of selection will sometimes necessitate a second visit to the shop in question.

Dress agencies

Sometimes it's hard to tell from the professional window display that a dress agency is selling second-hand clothes. The shop name often provides the clue – Second Time Around, Second Glance, Déjà Vu are all typical examples. The shops themselves are often tucked away in side streets just off the main High Street or else at the cheaper end of the main shopping street. You can always check on local dress agencies in the Yellow Pages.

Women customers find dress agencies useful for both selling and buying. In addition to clothes, there may be hats, handbags, shoes and costume jewellery. Occasionally there are new bargains – manufacturers' samples or bankrupt stock items. Shops vary enormously, both in the quality of the clothes they sell and in their presentation.

Most proprietors are quite fussy about which garments they will accept for second-hand sale; not only must they be in tip-top condition and newly cleaned but also fashionable and readily saleable. They must also be for the correct season. Summer clothes are accepted in late spring; winter garments in autumn.

Most agencies operate on a percentage-of-sale basis, holding and keeping garments on their rails for a set period, usually a couple of months, which may be extended. If the goods do not sell, they will either be returned to you, or given to charity if not collected by an agreed date. Items for sale are usually listed on an agreement form which is signed by both parties. Dress agencies are a useful means of disposing of mistakes – garments which you never wear for one reason or another, or dresses you have simply got tired of. You will never recoup anything like the amount you paid for them but, rather than hoard unworn garments in a crowded wardrobe, you may prefer to put even a modest return to better use. You can, of course, specify a minimum price for a garment you wish to dispose of, but bear in mind that the dress agency has to add its own percentage. There is no point in pricing a garment out of the average customer's reach. The agency will usually advise on a reasonable price.

Some guidelines on value

Quality

Critical shoppers are frequently shocked at the shoddy workmanship in garments today compared with the standards of even a few years ago. Every year clothes cost more, yet their quality seems to diminish: the cut is skimpier, linings are few and far between, there are trailing threads, puckered seams and badly finished buttonholes.

It is vital to perform your own quality control. Apart from buttonholes and hems, other key factors include the following.

Zips should be lightweight, and concealed in a neat placket, which should lie flat.

Lining material should reflect the quality of the main fabric. Lining which is cheap and shoddy will shorten the life of the garment.

Where fabric is patterned, or striped or check, the patterns, the stripes or the check should match as closely as possible across the seams. An exact match at every seam may be too much to hope for, but if there is a rack of garments to choose from, you may able to pick out the one with the least obvious mismatch, particularly on noticeable areas like the sleeve and side seams.

Garments in light colours tend to look cheap unless they are made from a good quality fabric. So be prepared to pay more for light colours.

The labels inside the garment state the country of manufacture which can be an indication of quality. Some of the best mass-produced clothes are made in Germany. Fashion-house labels, however, can be confusing. Since German fashion design has an image problem, German fashion houses adopt French and Italian-sounding names like Mondi, Ouiset and Le Truc, all of which are enormously popular with British women. Finland is another country with a reputation for good design and quality manufacture.

Fit

The comfort of a garment makes a lot of difference to its lifespan. If it doesn't hang or sit right, if it's restrictive or tight when you move, it usually ends up hanging idle in the wardrobe, regardless of how much it cost. Fit is a very important aspect of value for money.

Always try on prospective purchases; even Marks & Spencer now has cubicles in response to customer demand. There are often queues to use them but a big advantage if you are retired is that you can choose to shop at quiet times when you won't feel rushed or harassed by other shoppers.

When trying on a garment, lift up your arms, move around and sit down if possible. Sitting down is particularly important where both skirts and trousers are concerned; it's only by sitting that you can test for pulling. Older men, whose waist and hip measurement are often close, may achieve a more comfortable fit and better hang by wearing braces. Ladies could borrow this tip for skirts.

Never feel that you have to make an immediate decision. Just because you have tried on a garment which seems to fit reasonably well doesn't mean you have to buy it there and then. You can always come back. In the meantime, ask yourself whether you could do better elsewhere. It's only by assessing the comparative fit of different garments that you acquire a set of standards.

The garment should always look right for the size you are now, not when (and if) you lose a couple of pounds, or do some waist-reducing exercises, or wear something else with it, or take it up a couple of inches. Take into account, however, that you may well be an inch or two bigger after meals.

What about when you can't try clothes on, as is the case with men's shirts, for example? When you gain or lose weight, your neck size may change. Collar size is the most crucial measurement for a ready-made shirt, so it makes sense to check your neck measurement before going shopping, or get a sales assistant to do it for you. Be careful with slim-line shirts, however, which fit at the neck but don't meet in the middle. If this is your problem, look out for standard sizing. For men who aren't a standard size, a shopping-by-post shirt specialist, James Meade Shirts Limited, offers a range of seven sleeve sizes. The address is on page 145.

Everyone should check their measurements before going clothes shopping. Never try to cram yourself into too small a size, or compromise with a size too large. Depending on the garment, an easy hang is preferable to a glove-like fit, so do try to avoid an 'upholstered' look!

If you have to return a garment to a shop, do this as soon as possible. This may give you an improved chance of exchanging the garment for a bigger or smaller size while there is still adequate stock. Always keep the receipt. Marks & Spencer and branches of the John Lewis Partnership have always been the most accommodating of shops for returning goods, but even they tend to require the original proof of purchase. Without this, you will have to make do with credit vouchers instead of your cash.

Look before you buy

The best time to look for clothes or shoes is when the new season's stock first appears and there is maximum choice. You might find it useful to go shopping with your notebook rather than your cheque book at least for a first expedition. Shop around, jotting down details of places and prices. It is often helpful to try garments on and make comparisons. Take sample snippets from favourite garments with you so you can coordinate colours better. Snippets can be carefully cut from the seam allowance or hems, kept in an envelope or put on a safety pin.

If you look back on past purchases in years gone by, you'll no doubt recall with a wry smile more than one particular buy for which you paid what seemed over the odds at the time. Very likely that very same garment was still earning its keep many years later. There's many an extravagance which has never been regretted; and many a so-called bargain which had a rather short life.

Rather than shudder at a price tag, apply the theory of cost effectiveness. For example, a well fitting, carefully chosen, versatile jacket which might cost a three-figure sum can be better value for money than a much cheaper buy which never feels quite right anywhere. Cost it out on the basis of the number of times you may wear the garment over a period of years.

When not to buy

It is never wise to buy when you're in a hurry and haven't time to appraise a garment objectively. A typical example is when you're anxious to find something for a specific occasion at short notice. That way you will probably end up paying either too much or too little for something that you wear only once or twice and doesn't fit in with the rest of your wardrobe. If you update your wardrobe and accessories regularly and routinely on a seasonal basis you won't be thrown by special occasions. Equally don't buy when the decision is dependent on the price, for example in a sale. The criterion should always be, do you like it enough to have bought it anyhow? When in doubt, leave it alone.

Shopping in sales

Sales shopping is for the strong-minded, those who know exactly where they have gaps in their wardrobe and can make a quick and sure decision when they see what they want. Ditherers and impulse buyers are safer staying at home.

Good sales bargains are timeless classics, chosen with the same care and consideration given to normal clothes buying. The sales atmosphere of 'grab it while it's there' is the opposite of the good shopping techniques necessary for coordinated dressing. In fact, many shoppers find that sales get in the way of selective buying. Sales nowadays seem to start earlier, they drag on longer and are interspersed with mid-season reductions. Such frequent sales can even inhibit regular buying. Who wants to pay £x for something which may well be reduced within the month?

Before falling for a sale bargain, you should ask yourself why the garment has been left on the rails in the first place. Consider the following:

- *its flexibility:* how versatile is it? Is it a round-the-year item or a one-short-season-only buy, like an over-warm, heavyweight sweater or cardigan?
- *its compatibility:* will the potential purchase co-exist with at least two other items in your wardrobe? A difficult colour may be the reason why something ends up on the sales rack.

- *its washability:* if the garment is made of suede or any other dry-clean-only fabric, how much of a bargain is it? Is that what put off potential buyers?

Having given these warnings on the risks of sales fever, it is only fair to acknowledge that bargains can be found by discriminating shoppers who keep their head. There are sources where discounted 'designer' or 'big name' clothes can be found, often in areas near to the rag trade and often in short-let or end-of-lease premises.

Clothes care and maintenance

All in a lifetime

The over-50s are a generation brought up to look after their clothes, to hang them up properly after wear and to expect long service from them. Some older readers will have lived in households where there was domestic help with laundry and ironing. Others may recall being in domestic service themselves, looking after an employer's clothes as part of the job.

Clothes care originally involved moth balls, lavender bags and lots of white tissue paper. Winter heavyweights were packed away during the summer months and anxiously examined in the autumn for tell-tale holes. Cotton dresses were not seen again from autumn until the following May.

During the 1939–45 war years, clothes care meant make-do and mend. Worn collars and cuffs were unpicked and replaced; old jumpers were unravelled, the wool tied in skeins and the kinks washed out before the recycled wool was knitted into yet another smaller jumper, often striped with other oddments of wool. Women made blouses out of old parachutes, dyeing or fabric printing the material first. In second-hand nostalgia shops the old utility mark, which was once an indication of basic quality, is now a valuable clue for period dating.

Clothes care in the synthetic sixties when many people had washing machines became a matter of drip-dry, easy care and minimum iron with non-shrink acrylics replacing wool. The very easy-wash, quick-dry qualities of these new wonder fabrics with new names tended to outweigh the fact that they were often cold and clammy to the touch, and didn't hang or drape in the same way as natural fibres.

Today, natural fibres like wool, cotton, linen and silk are enjoying renewed popularity. They are often mixed with a small proportion of synthetic material, in order to prevent shrinkage and creasing. It has become impossible to guess the composition of a textile just by feeling it; you need to read the label carefully. You can ascertain how much a fabric is likely to crease by crushing it in your hand and watching whether it springs back to its original state.

The care label

Whether a garment is washable or not may well affect your decision to buy it or not since dry-cleaning will add substantially to the long-term cost. Sometimes this is unavoidable. You would expect to dry-clean a jacket; skirts and trousers, however, are made in washable fabric mixes, and these are worth a deliberate search.

Easier washability means you can choose lighter, brighter clothes. Colours or dark patterns used to be preferred because they didn't show the dirt. Few adults today wear clothes until they actually show visible signs of dirt. Today's standards of personal hygiene should mean that no garment is ever hung in the wardrobe unwashed. Even an item worn once will carry body odour. Many people, who are fastidious about personal freshness are sometimes remiss in this respect.

Remember to look at a garment's care label:

- before every wash, in case it says hand wash only
- for the correct temperature
- after washing, but before drying, in case it is not suitable for the tumble drier
- before you iron, for the correct heat setting.

So many of the limp garments sent to jumble sales are sad victims of carelessness in the wash.

Dry-cleaning

A care label which reads 'Dry-clean only' is clear enough, and usually applies to tailored coats, jackets, suits with interlinings and certain fabrics which may run or shrink.

Sometimes, however, the label reads 'Dry-cleaning recommended'. This may depend on the type of garment and whether there are shoulder pads, interfacings or linings involved. Sometimes the garment needs steam pressing after a wash. In all these cases, it is safer to stick to dry-cleaning.

Occasionally, you will find that dry-cleaning is recommended even when the fabric is clearly marked as cotton or some other equally washable material. The recommendation may be given because the garment manufacturer is playing safe in the light of inadequate information from the fabric supplier. A careful handwash in lukewarm water will usually suffice, although you do this at your own risk.

Storing and hanging

Check regularly that you are making the most of existing wardrobe space; some garments such as shirts and blouses only need half-length hanging room. You may have room to add an extra hanging rack to take advantage of this. Brochures of fitted wardrobe systems can give you ideas for converting existing cupboards and closets, which a DIY enthusiast might possibly copy. If you have sufficient floor space or access to a spare room, an additional free-standing portable garment rail can be useful for clothes which need airing or which are awaiting alteration.

Central heating and today's lightweight fabrics mean that more garments than ever are wearable and interchangeable between seasons. How much you pack and store away as summer or winter wear depends on the space you have available.

It can be valuable to 'rest' garments that you've worn many times recently. After a month or more, you may take them out and see them with fresh eyes – together with different accessories and new colours.

Some people like to group all garments of the same kind together in their wardrobes: jackets, shirts, and so on. Others prefer to group clothes by colour. Whatever your favoured system, your aim should be to see quickly the maximum number of potential mix and matches. Don't always wear the same old partners together – experiment. With an organised wardrobe, the most obvious gaps will quickly become apparent. Make a note of them, so that you can decide on priorities before you next go on a shopping trip.

Shoe care

- **D**on't wear the same pair of shoes day in and day out. They lose their shape and can get very sloppy. Do alternate them with other pairs. When you 'rest' them, use shoe trees to preserve the shape.
- **D**on't break the backs of shoes by forcing them on. Use a shoe horn – long handled ones are particularly useful.
- **D**on't use a wire brush for suede shoes. A soft shoe brush is much kinder.
- **D**o clean shoes while they're still warm from wear and the leather is soft.
- **N**ew suede shoes or boots should be sprayed with Scotchguard before wearing to provide extra protection from dirt and the weather.
- **N**ew leather shoes should be cleaned before wearing them outdoors and before they get dirty.
- **T**ight-fitting shoes can be eased by spraying inside with an aerosol shoe stretcher.
- **R**epairs, where necessary, should always be undertaken immediately.

The following are a couple of tips for high-heel wearers.

High heels often have badly scuffed dents in the leather. The loose leather should be carefully eased and smoothed out, and the torn material gently stuck back with clear nail varnish.

High heels can get horribly stained when they sink into grass. Wear flat-heeled shoes or sandals wherever possible but for special outdoor events, like garden parties where a special outfit needs high heels, you can protect the heels by covering them in sellotape. Do it carefully and no one will ever know it's there!

Recommended gadgets

Attention to detail can make a lot of difference to how we look. Often, finding just the right product or gadget can solve a problem.

Using a sleeveboard when ironing avoids an ugly sleeve crease.

Fluff and 'pilling' can be removed from a sweater with a battery-operated gadget called a lint shaver.

Iron-on bonding provides a quick and easy way of shortening hems and sleeves. 'Wundaweb' is a well-known proprietary brand and widely available. It's also useful for invisibly mending small tears.

Readily-removeable shoulder pads can be bought in all sizes with velcro attachments which slip under bra straps.

Sloppy sweater or cardigan sleeves can be made to fit more closely and neatly at the wrists by using men's armbands, or wrist bands made of elastic.

Haberdashery departments are happy hunting grounds for new ideas and products. Occasionally the resulting find may turn out to be disappointingly gimmicky; other items will make you wonder what you ever did without them. So keep on trying.

A couple of plastic inflatable coat hangers are useful for drip-drying shirts and blouses because they imitate the natural rounded shoulderline. They are also ideal for airing sweaters and cardigans. Experimenting with different kinds of hangers for different garments is also a matter of trial and error. One person's perfect tie rack is another's white elephant. Try to discover what works best in your wardrobe.

ACHIEVING A TOTAL LOOK

**STYLE IS A SIMPLE WAY
OF SAYING COMPLICATED THINGS**

Jean Cocteau

■

Accessories – after the facts

'Accessories' is the word commonly used to include all those items of dress like shoes, bags, belts, jewellery, scarves and so on. For men it means ties, belts and watches.

Maybe it's the semantic confusion surrounding the word 'accessory' which makes many older dressers still regard these items as extra add-ons, after-thoughts, rather than essential elements of the whole look. 'Accessory' normally means contributing to, or secondary, not the most important part. This certainly isn't true where clothes are concerned. Detail is always an integral part of design.

Think of detail in relation to period architecture or furniture design. While overall shape and proportion matter, the functional aspects and how these are expressed are of equal importance. In the case of a house, think of doors, windows and chimney pots; in the case of furniture, look at locks, fastenings, handles and castors. Not only are these details all part of the whole, they are the areas where designers add their individual, often recognisable, flourishes. It is in this sense that accessories are the details of dress. They deserve more thought and attention than they usually receive.

As fashion design becomes more generally accepted as an art form, each of us, in our own small way, has the means of self-expression and creativity through the way we wear our clothes. Accessories are very important. They are our personal signature.

Mix and coordinate

All this is a far cry from the days when a man's belt was seen as a means of holding up his trousers rather than a visual statement. However, if men were guilty of not bothering, women's error was to try too hard. After buying any new outfit, the next step was to search for a matching bag and shoes; and matching in those days *meant* matching. Gloves, too, had to 'match' and endless, obsessive hours were spent trailing from shop to shop, worrying assistants with requests to be allowed to take an item to the door or window so as to peer more minutely at the colour in the daylight.

The good news is that accessories don't have to match any more, but they do have to blend (see photographs on page 69). Coordination is the key, and this is much harder to define, although it's obvious when it works. There's always the incentive to go on trying and improving the end result. Two vital aspects of coordination are proportion and colour. Keep contrast under control. If more than two accessories are in a contrasting colour to the main garment, you will end up with a spotty effect, a bittiness which will spoil the overall look.

Develop a sense of proportion

Make a habit of using a full-length mirror whenever you try on clothes together with accessories – so much depends on proportion, and you need to train your eye. It may sound silly, but it's only in front of a full-length mirror that you can judge hats and even earrings. It will come easier if you get into the habit of asking questions: Is this wide-brimmed hat too near my padded shoulderline? Does this A-line skirt look less squat with a slight heel rather than with flat pumps?

When you have put an outfit together, it will be immediately obvious if you've got it right. It should feel comfortable, a well-integrated whole. To save trying-on time in future, jot down the combination, right to the last detail, so that the look is instantly accessible the next time you need it. You may feel sure you'll remember it, but the chances are you won't, and on the next occasion you may need to dress in a hurry without time to experiment. How you record the information is up to you: sticky labels on the inside door of the wardrobe, a card-index system or a notebook are all possibilities.

The trick of keeping costume jewellery in proportion is to try on a variety of different items – beads, brooches and so on – and then remove them one at a time. If the outfit looks incomplete without the item you've just removed, replace it. If in doubt, leave it off. A general guideline is to wear like with like; for example, tiny, delicate earrings with a fragile necklace; big dramatic earrings with a chunky brooch. Don't mix the incompatible.

Hemlines

Gone are the days when fashion dictated that hemlines had to be x inches in relation to the knee. Hemlines are variable. The best place for most hemlines is where they best suit your proportions and your individual leg shape. Here's a simple general test to determine this:

1. Take a large bath towel and stand in front of a full-length mirror.
2. Hold the bath towel up in front of you widthways.
3. Raise and lower the bottom edge to see the difference it makes to the shape of your calves.
4. Decide on the most flattering level.

You can do this exercise twice, once wearing high heels and once with low heels. The line may or may not vary. Don't forget to make a note of the length, so that you can adjust most of your hemlines accordingly.

Another factor influencing hemlines is the shape and fluidity of the skirt fabric. A slim straight skirt can be worn shorter whereas a full or flared skirt in a floating fabric looks flattering worn longer.

Colour harmony

Anyone who has attended a session on colour analysis (see p 30) will find coordinated shopping much easier than before. Your most suitable range of basic and neutral colours, which include those appropriate for bags and shoes, will have been identified and simplified. The range of colour combinations from your personal palette will harmonise because they originate from the same colour family. (Much of this know-how can be gained from reading some of the books about colour analysis and wardrobe planning which are listed on page 147.)

The more you learn about coordination, the more carefully chosen will be your future accessory purchases. You will inevitably choose quality, not quantity. Your mistakes will be fewer. In fact, you may end up as the beneficiary of other people's mistakes by paying regular visits to dress agencies and charity shops. Accessory bargains include quality gloves, silk scarves, and leather handbags which respond well to a good renovating polish, provided the linings and clasp are intact. The post-Christmas period is a good time to find silk ties.

Bags and belts

Although new bags and belts may cost as much as a basic garment – and this is a tough, new idea to get used to – their lifespan is long and they will be worn in conjunction with many future garments. Try to look on them as an investment. They are highly acceptable birthday and Christmas presents, provided you can do the choosing! Make a list of missing accessories and start dropping some heavy hints to the family.

Shopping for a quality woman's fashion belt can be a problem, particularly in a big size. However, a large waist can be flattered by an interesting buckle or decorative detail at the front, even if the rest is hidden by a jacket. A Yorkshire firm, Liv-in Leather (see p 146), runs a mail order service for a selection of soft leather belts made to any measurement in a variety of colours.

The Liv-in range of bags includes a wrist bag for men, quite commonplace in Europe and useful for carrying keys, cash and credit cards. Your average older British male may need time and a little persuasion to get used to the idea of carrying a bag; as an initial introduction you could buy a cheaper version.

A handbag has to be functional as well as attractive. Beware of bags which are heavy even when empty, and do resist the temptation to carry round more belongings than you need. There's nothing more associated with muddle-headedness than a woman rummaging in her bag. As we grow less sharp-sighted and our fingers lose their dexterity, what's called for is a lightweight, unlined bag in which money, keys and train ticket are easily accessible without the need to fumble.

Taken-for-granted accessories

Functional items like glasses and watches are now fashion accessories in their own right. Maybe yours need an update or at least a review.

Most older people wear glasses at least some of the time, usually for reading small print. If you wear glasses all the time, however, it's unlikely that the same pair will be appropriate for wearing with the range of different outfits in your wardrobe. There is a huge range of frames available today, so before your next eye test and before you select your next new pair of glasses, check through your wardrobe before deciding on the frames. For women who wear glasses all or most of the time, eye shadow is a great enhancer, chosen with the frame colour in mind.

There's more to buying a watch than wanting an accurate means of telling the time. For men, some brands of watch are expensive status symbols – if that is what you want. There is, too, a growing interest in both men's and women's quality second-hand watches, dating back to the pre-quartz era. However, there may well be occasions when wearing an expensive watch poses a theft risk – in the changing rooms at the swimming baths or sports centre, for example, or perhaps on holiday. Nowadays you can find a range of much cheaper 'fun' watches – sports watches as well as evening watches. This type of watch, worn with a light-coloured strap looks much more attractive with summer wear than the conventional watch with its dark leather strap, and a small detail like this can really give a lift to your appearance.

Shoes

Most High Street shoe shops are owned by the British Shoe Corporation which sells one in four of the million or so shoes sold each week in the UK. Its holding includes Freeman, Hardy & Willis, Cable & Co, Bertie, Trueform, Manfield, Dolcis, Saxone, Lilley & Skinner, Shoe City, Curtess and Roland Cartier.

Anyone wanting shoes which are larger, smaller, wider or narrower than the absolute average has to hunt further afield. For men this needn't be a shoe shop; High and Mighty, the main men's retail outsize clothing chain, stocks shoe sizes 11–15. It also has a mail order service (see p 145).

Styles that fit and flatter

Finding good quality stylish shoes which fit well is much more of a problem for older women. For anyone other than the mythical Mrs Average, it can be difficult and time-consuming trying to find shoes which have the correct width, depth and length. Narrow shoes are elusive; wide fittings are more easily available but so many UK brands look hopelessly old-fashioned.

Good fit and comfort count above all, and remember shoe stress and foot discomfort show in our faces. Some people find that suede 'gives', providing a high level of soft comfort. However, no one wants to ruin the overall appearance of a carefully chosen ageless outfit with a pair of matronly shoes. Classic court shoes with a not-too-high heel, and low-heeled classic pumps are the most versatile shoes, but these can be the hardest styles to find.

When you go shopping for shoes, grit your teeth and make the following resolutions:

- I will not sacrifice comfort and fit for the sake of appearance
- I will not accept the fuddy-duddy
- I am looking for shoes which fit as well as flatter.

You may need to seek out a specialist shoe shop, one which provides a measuring service and keeps a good stock of stylish shoes in a variety of fittings, often imported from Italy or Germany.

Specialist shops

If you write to the Society of Shoe Fitters (see p 146), enclosing a stamped self-addressed envelope, you will be sent a list of its members and the shops where they work.

Specialist shops generally provide a personal shoe fitting service for men as well as women. They will often keep a card-index record of your exact requirements; they will advise on the type and brand of shoe most suitable for your feet, and they may send a reminder postcard when these are next in stock.

You will probably have to reconcile yourself to spending a significant proportion of your budget on shoes, at least in winter. In summer there are inexpensive alternatives such as trainers, sandals, moccasins, espadrilles and so on, which help to make your wardrobe more versatile. These are not suitable in the winter months.

The British Footwear Manufacturers Federation, (see p 144) publishes an inexpensive booklet called *Footwear for Special Needs,* which includes unusual sizes, mail order services, orthopaedic shoes as well as made-to-measure, both for everyday wear and for special occasions such as weddings. They even have a made-to-measure service using fabric to match your outfit. Their listing also includes firms who provide an odd size shoe service for people with one foot a different size from the other. An average price guide is given for each service.

Stockings and tights

Nothing ladders more easily than tights which are too tight. An extra-wide fitting solves this problem. Maternity tights, too, have plenty of 'give' and now come in all weights and colours. When you do find a brand which is a good fit as well as a flattering shade, you can save money by buying multi-packs. This also gives the advantage of matching up when only one leg has laddered. Odd stockings can be paired, of course, but the same principle can be applied to two pairs of otherwise spoiled tights. Just cut off the laddered legs, switch the tights around if necessary so that you have a right and a left and wear the two pairs, one on top of the other.

Tights and stockings need to be practical, serviceable and comfortable to wear, but they must also complement the rest of your appearance. So many women choose tights or stockings in yesterday's shades, reminiscent of the fawn lisle stockings worn by Nora Batty. The use of Lycra has made sheer hosiery almost an everyday possibility, especially for wearing with summer dresses. Sheer and opaque hosiery comes in many neutral shades including navy, grey and ivory. Department stores usually have an excellent selection of tones, textures and colours. If you suffer from aching legs and feet you may be interested in the advice about support hosiery on page 87.

Individual touches

Yesterday's storehouse

If you are a hoarder, and have lived for many years in the same house, you may well be sitting on a treasure trove of interesting accessories, stored away items which are now more 'wearable' than you'd ever imagined they could be when you packed them up. Sometimes, when older relatives die, their houses have to be cleared in a hurry, and personal effects may get stowed away in a box to be sorted out at a later date, or never. So take a second look through drawers, cupboards and, possibly, the loft.

What counted as almost worthless dressing-up-box items a few years ago may be valued additions to today's wardrobe, not necessarily in their original form, but adapted or altered for present-day use; far better for Aunt Rose's bits and pieces to live again than for them to fade and wither away. Old lace, buckles, artificial flowers, evening bags, yesterday's costume jewellery and watches are all highly sought after today.

From other sources

In most towns there are nostalgia shops or stalls selling all kinds of period clothes right up to and including those from the 1960s. Antique markets and jumble sales may also be happy hunting grounds. You need to be restrained and highly selective about buying from these sources. Avoid anything faded, or anything that droops. The bedraggled look will not become you.

Most women's clothes from the 1960s will be too short to wear today but could be a good source for high quality buttons if the garment is cheap enough. Keep an eye open for this kind of detail in charity shops. Replacing boring chainstore buttons with a classier or more original alternative is a well-known way of transforming a garment. Button Box (see p 144), in London's Covent Garden, has a wonderful selection of buttons in all shapes and sizes. The store also provides a full-colour mail order catalogue. Its address is on page 144, along with that of Button Queen, another London shop with a wide range which includes antique buttons.

Another button idea from America is Click-its, which clip on to existing buttons. Sold by leading department stores, they have 200 different designs available in sets of six. They are not cheap – but the most expensive are limited editions.

Ethnic scarves and jewellery of variable quality can be found on market stalls in towns and cities. Such merchandise can be cheap and look good, but be selective – you don't want to look like a third-age fortune-teller! The peacock colours of silk scarves are very attractive and are often a fraction of shop prices.

Charity shops don't only sell second-hand clothing. Those like Oxfam which raise funds for Third World countries also sell imported items including bags and jewellery. Try and develop the skill of seeing items out of their immediate context and visualising them with your own garments.

The British Museum may not seem the obvious place to go shopping for an unusual brooch or pair of earrings, but – along with many other museums today – it produces authentic copies of ancient jewellery which is sold in the museum shop. The Crafts Council runs a section within the shop at the Victoria and Albert Museum. It sells contemporary design work, including jewellery. The Council also publishes a countrywide Crafts Map which lists selected independent shops and galleries selling high-quality work. This provides the opportunity to combine possible shopping with a leisurely day out. You can write for the Crafts Map, enclosing a stamped addressed envelope, at the address on page 144.

Using your own creativity

Knitting

Knitting is by far the most popular craft practised by women generally, and by older women in particular. Since it's not a rare skill among the over-50s, knitting tends to be taken for granted and undervalued by this age group. Many experienced knitters could review and refresh their worthwhile skills. Rather than routinely following patterns for very ordinary-looking garments, they may well be able to achieve a far more ambitious and fashion-conscious garment (see photograph on page 34). It's worth noting that young knitwear designers often rely on the skills of older knitters, not only to make up their original designs, but also to advise on which stitches work best in which yarns.

If you don't wish to try your hand at design, you can buy books of designer knitwear patterns. A decent library will show you the kinds of books that are now available. Rowan, the Yorkshire quality yarn suppliers, compile kits of styles specially commissioned each season from top knitwear designers. Rowan's illustrated kits leaflet and pattern magazines, as well as their yarns, are obtainable by mail order from Wool Works at the address on page p146. Other makers of kits advertise widely in weekend newspapers and the like.

Knitting is by no means an exclusively female craft. Knitting machines have revived male interest and encouraged male acceptance of the hobby, rather like microwave ovens have persuaded more men to interest themselves in cooking. The Bishop of Leicester is just one well-known knitter who has written books on the subject and, of course, the Canadian Kaffe Fassett has had an exhibition of his exclusive designs at the V&A!

Sewing

Daytime dressmaking classes and home tailoring are popular subjects in adult education centres. Finishing touches such as belts, buttons and zips can always be made up professionally if you feel you haven't the necessary expertise. If you shy away from pattern cutting, women's magazines frequently have 'cut-out' garment special offers. It is also possible to buy half-finished garments which only require one seam to be sewn and the hem to be finished. Liberty's 'ready-to-sew' skirts have a ruched elasticated waist and come in a variety of fabrics, including velvet, taffeta and shot silk for evening wear. These skirts, as well as tops, are obtainable at any of Liberty's 19 branches, or by mail order from the London store.

Other crafts

Crochet, lace making, embroidery and quilting can all be put to good use to add original touches to clothes. Belts, bags, collars and waistcoats are all possibilities; the results don't have to look 'folksy'. Once you are familiar with the technicalities of an individual craft, you can translate this into modern design. You may be familiar with the basics of a craft already, or you may be starting from scratch as an absolute beginner. Sometimes you can be fortunate in finding an individual teacher; alternatively, classes are often run by the local adult education service or Women's Institute. Why not see what's on offer? Almost anything is possible: lovely scarves are produced by silk screen printing classes while students in silversmithing classes may learn to make and repair their own jewellery.

Most adult education centres hold regular exhibitions to show off their students' practical work, sometimes on their own premises, and occasionally in public libraries. If you live in the country, look out for the Women's Institute stand at local county shows. There, too, you will find a display of practical work from local classes.

BODY CARE

THE BODY NEVER LIES
Martha Graham

■

How to stay fit, active and attractive

Appearance, health and fitness are all inextricably linked. Just as a vintage car needs regular maintenance to keep the engine functioning and purring away happily, as well as to preserve the bodywork, so too does the older human body require regular and sustained attention, inside and out. Our bodywork may well have suffered some damage in the past as a result of bad habits such as over-indulgence or smoking or basic neglect, such as insufficient exercise. It's never too late to decide on a rescue job or regular maintenance from now on.

The average person in their late 50s can look forward confidently to many more years of life. Remaining fit, active and attractive for as long as possible will greatly enhance the quality of those years. The time couldn't be better for anyone of any age who is interested in improving their health, fitness or appearance; society is now more body-conscious than ever before.

Health and fitness clubs and centres, gyms and lidos are mushrooming. So, too, are High Street beauty enterprises offering toning and tanning, as well as more scientific-sounding skin treatments. Many establishments are franchises, run by the untrained and unqualified, so you will need to shop around and select services with care (see p 90). In the meantime there is a great deal we can do to look after our bodies on a DIY basis.

Watching your weight

Weighing more than you should when you're older not only spoils your appearance, but also brings increased health risks from diabetes, heart disease and varicose veins. You may feel perfectly healthy, but carrying around excess weight puts additional stress on joints which may suffer later from arthritis. The time to take action is now.

Being overweight is the result of an imbalance between calorie intake and energy output. The best way to correct the situation is by reviewing and amending existing habits. Try eating less from a more balanced and varied diet, at the same time as taking more exercise. This two-way approach won't bring instant results, but you will certainly see and feel the benefits in six months' time.

Guidelines for healthier eating

Your aim should be to reduce fat, sugar and salt in your diet and to eat more fibre-rich foods. Try to adopt some new shopping habits.

To reduce fat:

- buy low-fat spreads rather than butter
- use skimmed or semi-skimmed milk
- buy low-fat yoghurt, not cream
- buy more fish and chicken.

To reduce sugar:

- cut out cakes, chocolate, crisps, biscuits and puddings
- buy unsweetened fruit juices and plenty of fresh fruit
- look out for 'hidden' sugar in ingredient lists where it is called sucrose, glucose, dextrose, fructose or honey.

To reduce salt:
- buy fewer preserved foods like ham, sausages, bacon, beefburgers and pâté, all of which contain salt as well as fat
- buy a range of herbs and spices to use as alternative flavourings to salt.

To increase fibre:
- buy more fresh fruit and vegetables
- choose wholemeal bread and wholegrain breakfast cereals
- try different kinds of beans and lentils.

The following good cooking habits are part of healthy eating:
- grill rather than fry
- eat potatoes boiled or baked, not roasted or as chips
- if you do fry, always use a non-stick pan with minimal vegetable oil, preferably cold-pressed
- always drain excess fat from mince and other meats
- remove the skin from chicken.

There is no shortage of leaflets and posters telling us the kind of foods we should be eating to keep ourselves fit. Theory and practice, however, are not the same thing. What you know you should be eating and what you actually are eating are two different things. As an experiment, try keeping a food diary for a week to check on your true eating habits. Only then will you be able to judge if changes need to be made.

Outside help with weight loss

Be wary of any commercial organisation which advertises rapid weight loss by way of diets or diet foods. What you should be aiming for is a permanent weight reduction which can only come about through a change in your eating habits. If you are very overweight and feel you can't achieve this on your own, consider contacting Weight Watchers (see p 146). Local sessions are held all over the country giving group support and regular weight checks. There are reduced rates for the over-60s. Members can choose the pace at which they want to lose weight by opting for one of three diet levels. There is a food plan for vegetarians and the programme also includes an exercise plan. For those unable to attend a class, there is a service called Weight Watchers by Mail, the details of which are given on page 140.

It is worth discussing a diet with your GP first, however, before committing yourself to the expense of Weight Watchers. Many health practices are now offering additional health promotion services. The practice nurse may be prepared to weigh you on a weekly or monthly basis and supply a diet sheet, as well as moral support.

Eating: more than just food

It may seem trite to declare that eating is an important activity to us all – and yet it is. Think how dull the days are when for reasons of sickness we have to avoid food; the day stretches ahead without interest. Meals are a daily highlight.

At its best, eating is an enjoyable social activity. It also gives a great deal of sensory pleasure; aesthetically – in the way a table and a meal look – as well as in the more evident areas of smell and taste. These are important and yet undervalued aspects of eating. To encourage and sustain the good eating habits which will keep your weight down and lead to healthy skin and hair, they deserve more attention than they currently receive.

Food, drink and the kitchen sink

The reality of everyday life is that we don't just consume fats and fibre, calories, vitamins and minerals and so on, we eat food – fresh, frozen, fast and even junk from time to time. The quality of the meals we eat and the pleasure they give us vary enormously according to the amount of energy and effort we put into their preparation, and the mood we are in.

During our working lives there may be little spare time for a creative approach to cooking and many people get into a slightly monotonous routine,

▲ Accessories in shades that blend, tone on tone, with an outfit, give the elegant, streamlined 'total look'.

◄ Bright accents lift dark colours but two blobs of any one contrast colour are enough. Either match other accessories to your outfit or go for a second contrast shade.

▶ It's a pity to shun jeans as too young and casual – dark ones can look especially elegant teamed with a great cardigan or shirt.

▲ A comfortable tracksuit is cut out for the senior lifestyle and can be stylish too. Look for long loose tops in bright but soft colours.

▶ Casuals with good shape and colour sense look smart in the informal way that's ideal for the over-50s. The bright bomber jacket and ski pants shown here are good examples.

▼ After applying moisturizer and light foundation over face with a sponge, gently brush minimal amount of concealer on any dark shadows around the eyes, patting it into the skin with finger. Avoid eye bags, but use lightly on marks or high colour round nose and on cheeks.

▼ Put three dots of cream blush on 'apple' of cheeks and blend towards ear with fingertips, eliminating 'stripes'. Keep blusher out of crows' feet. Apply loose colourless powder to centre of face and around lips by pressing lightly with powder puff to set make-up. Brush away excess.

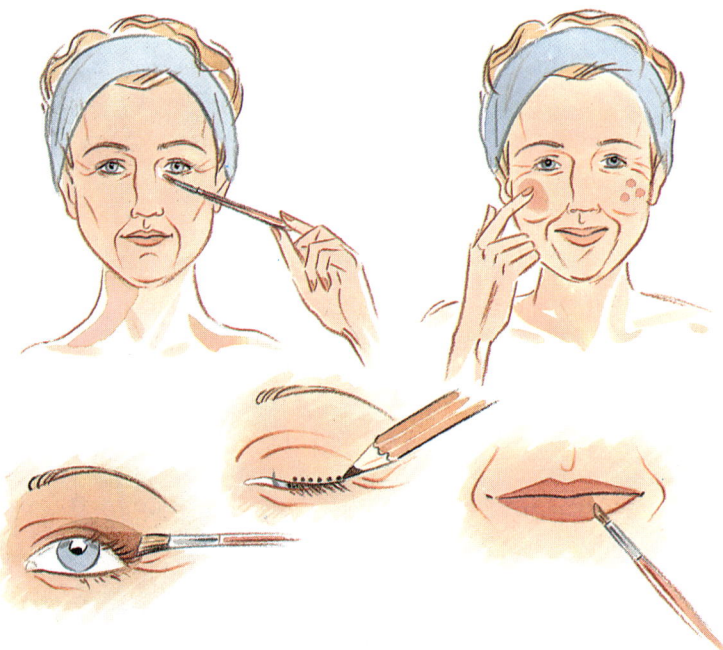

▲ Brush light matt eyeshadow half way up outer section of upper lid, creating a soft triangle. Brush in second slightly warmer shade at outer corner of the upper lid giving the eye a lift. Keep away from 'droop' at outer corners of eyes.

▲ Dot brown or light charcoal eyeline next to top and bottom lashes with a soft shadow pencil, then smudge it in with fingertips or a foam applicator. Don't extend beyond the eye. Apply two coats of brown or dark blue mascara to lashes, allowing each coat to dry and removing any clogs before next application.

▲ Relax but close lips and, working from centre to corners, draw in mouth with lipliner to tone with lipstick. Soften edges with fingertip and blot before applying lipstick with brush. Powder the edges to set.

possibly buying a lot of convenience foods. Retirement is a good time to do things differently.

Many women enjoy cooking; it only becomes a chore when they are responsible for meals, day in and day out. Job-sharing begins at home and there are many opportunities nowadays for men to discover or improve their culinary skills, perhaps via television programmes or local adult education classes. Microwave cooking seems to have a particular appeal for men, as does slow cooking.

For people who live alone, it's easy to lose interest in food preparation and so much simpler to make do with a snack or a sandwich.

Variety is the spice

Many people agree that there's nothing quite so enjoyable as a tasty meal, cooked by somebody else. Anticipation and the element of surprise are vital ingredients and all part of the pleasure.

Mealtimes can be made more enjoyable for yourself and others by turning them into an occasion now and again. This also provides a good excuse to dress up and take special care with our appearance. Looking good is a vital part of feeling good.

Vary the company

Eating solitary meals all the time is pretty uninspiring, and with one person in four living alone these days, it's an experience with which many are familiar. This will be the situation for increasing numbers of people unless they take steps to change it. Someone has to start the ball rolling with a first invitation to share a meal. It could be the first of many. It doesn't need to be anything more than a simple lunch of home-made soup, followed by cheese or salad. Alternatively, you could invite your next-door neighbour to a late breakfast of scrambled eggs one Sunday morning.

Couples, too, may feel the benefit of more varied social contacts at mealtimes. It's very easy for a relationship to become inward-looking, especially in retirement when couples inevitably become more dependent on each other for day-to-day companionship. You might feel you don't want to be bothered with the demands and expectations of formal entertaining, but making a conscious and deliberate effort to include others round the table at mealtimes from time to time keeps you in touch with the rest of the world. You may like to consider one of the following ideas:

- an informal supper, which gets over the business of asking only couples, a limiting and iniquitous custom which excludes and isolates so many interesting solo men and women
- an impromptu garden party or a summer barbecue; outdoor entertaining is equally informal
- an invitation to morning coffee or afternoon tea on the balcony or patio can be a friendly and spontaneous gesture which may be very much appreciated by someone who lives alone, or a newcomer to the area.

Vary the table

The visual appearance of food matters tremendously, not just when there are guests but when you are on your own. Anticipation is a great appetiser.

Few people dress for dinner these days but it is still worth taking trouble over an attractively-arranged table:

- vary cloths, napkins and crockery
- create your own original table decorations, from flowers or fruit perhaps
- eat by candlelight occasionally, it's restful as well as romantic.

Vary the menu

Being retired means three meals a day at home instead of one or two. Don't become a martyr to your kitchen. Make occasional use of the many available options, such as the following:

- takeaways are fun as an occasional treat. Alternatives include fish and chips, Chinese or Indian food, or pizza; some pizza places provide a free motorbike delivery service
- prepare a picnic to take to the park and eat it in the sunshine and fresh air along with the squirrels

- pub lunches are usually good value for money and are popular on weekdays. Many pubs also do reasonably priced Sunday lunches. These can be variable in quality so try to go by the recommendation of a like-minded friend or acquaintance
- get together with half a dozen gourmet friends and run your own up-market luncheon club, wine included. It could be done on a reciprocal rota basis once a week, or once a month, or by paying an agreed amount into a communal kitty.

Fluids are important

The body is composed mainly of water. Three to four pints of fluid are needed each day in order for it to carry out its many and varied functions. Approximately one pint of water a day is exhaled by the lungs in the process of breathing, and nearly another pint evaporates through the skin. Another major function of your water intake is to flush out the system through the kidneys and to get rid of waste products; constipation is a very lowering condition and can be aggravated by not drinking sufficient fluids. What you choose to drink in order to make up the body's water requirement is up to you; any mixture of healthy fluids will do, including wine or beer in moderation.

Sometimes men and women cut down on their fluids when they are older. They feel perhaps that they don't need so much liquid now that they seem to perspire less than in younger days. This is a fallacy; the body continues to sweat, however invisibly.

Another reason why older people sometimes deliberately limit their fluid intake is an exaggerated worry about going to the toilet too often, or not getting there in time. Help and advice is available for this problem (see p 136). Restricting fluids isn't the answer and can result in health problems which will lower your spirits and are far more difficult to address.

Alcohol

For most of us, the occasional glass of beer or wine, gin or whisky, is something we enjoy on social occasions. We associate alcohol with fun and relaxation; a contributory factor to feeling good. Let's not forget, however, that alcohol is a toxin. The average recommended guidelines for weekly alcohol consumption are 14 units for women and 21 units for men. One unit of alcohol comprises any one of the following alternatives: half a pint of lager, cider or beer; one glass of spirits; one glass of wine, sherry, port or Martini. However, these limits may be too high for some older people since tolerance to alcohol decreases significantly with age. The kidneys and the liver become less able to break down the alcohol. How much is safe for you to drink depends on your state of health and whether or not you are taking medication on a regular basis.

If there is a conflict between how much you want to drink and how much is safe for you to drink, help and information can be obtained from an alcohol advice and counselling agency. A local address and telephone number can be supplied by Alcohol Concern (see p 143), which publishes a series of leaflets called *Safer Drinking for the Over-60s* and includes *A DIY Guide for Older People*.

Smoking

Smoking is an undisputed long-term health risk. Statistics show it to be a major contributory factor in cancer, heart disease, circulatory problems, chronic bronchitis and emphysema. Just because you don't actually suffer from any or all of these conditions doesn't mean that smoking isn't affecting your daily fitness or continuing health into old age. Do you get out of breath easily when you run for a bus or climb the stairs? Do you suffer from a smoker's cough?

Smoking is an addiction which adversely affects other aspects of your life such as:

your appearance
social relationships
personal relationships.

Your appearance

The connection between smoking and face wrinkles has been studied by doctors since 1856. A recent report in the British Medical Journal showed how cigarette smokers could actually be distinguished from non-smokers on the basis of facial features. 'Smoker's face', a distinctive clinical sign or specific characteristic, is quickly and easily recognised by nurses and medical students. Other obvious signs apparent to everyone are nicotine-stained fingers and teeth. Smokers need to take extra care with frequent dental checks to safeguard against plaque.

Social relationships

The fact that smoking is now either restricted or prohibited in so many public places – on trains, in restaurants and shops – should be some indication of how unpleasant most non-smokers find a smoky atmosphere.

Smokers need to be more aware of how anti-social their habit is, especially when they are a guest in a non-smoker's home, or when they are sharing a lift in a car. Established friends may tolerate your habit but potential new friends may be put off by the smoke and odour which is absorbed by their clothes. Smoking can be a serious social disadvantage.

Personal relationships

Smoking has an impact on family relationships. Don't be seduced by toddlers who are fascinated by a grandfather who puffs out smoke, especially from a pipe. The children's parents may not be so delighted with the habit, particularly if there is a baby in the house. These days even the youngest children are taught at school about the dangers of smoking as part of their health education, and it can be confusing and upsetting for them to be confronted with conflicting messages. Young children experience worry and concern when parents or grandparents smoke.

Finally, what about your partner? Family members may loathe the fug and messy ashtrays but still love the smoker. Yet how far are you pushing your luck and your partner's tolerance and goodwill? It isn't easy to sit back and watch someone you love ruining their health. What about the risks to your partner? There is increasing evidence about the dangers of passive or secondary smoking in public places; how much greater must be the dangers in the smaller confines of a home.

Single smokers in search of a new partner via a lonely hearts column, computer dating or introduction agency will notice the frequent request – non-smoker preferred.

When you really want to stop

It is never too late to stop smoking. Everyone knows somebody who stopped despite years of smoking. You may need help; there is plenty available.

QUIT, the National Society of Non-Smokers (see p 146) has a telephone counselling line. Counsellors, often ex-smokers themselves, are available to talk and listen, and they can tell you whether there are support services near you. QUIT also has a sequence of recorded messages by Claire Rayner, one for each weekday, with tips to help you through the early stages of giving up. QUIT also runs smoking courses once a month in the London area. Other people to ask for advice and help are your GP, health centre or health authority.

The smoking habit may be part of a bigger problem. Sometimes people smoke to take their mind off constant pain like arthritis, for instance, or the emotional pain of bereavement or loss. The dependency may have originated as a means of coping with anxiety. Acupuncture and hypnotherapy have both proved helpful to people prepared to make a high personal commitment. Always be sure to seek a reputable practitioner. The Institute of Complementary Medicine (see p 145) has a list of registered practitioners in both acupuncture and hypnotherapy.

Exercise

A regular programme of movement and activity will keep you feeling more supple and looking more youthful. No matter what age you begin, before long you should start noticing improvements in some of the following areas.

The way you stand and walk: you will be less likely to slouch and you will be aware of what it feels like to 'walk tall'.

The way you carry your clothes: your shoulders will lose their stiffness and your movements will be more fluid. Balance and coordination will also improve.

Your complexion: exercise increases circulation to the skin and improves its colour.

Your body shape: you may well be able to get into clothes which had become too tight. Since exercise helps to burn up calories, it can help keep weight in check over a sustained period of time.

Your exercise routine doesn't have to be anything as strenuous as jogging or aerobics. Ideally, it should be natural, gentle and non-competitive. You can make a small start today by getting into the following habits:

- walk, rather than take the bus
- collect your daily newspaper, instead of having it delivered
- leave the car at home more frequently
- climb stairs in shops and offices, instead of using escalators and lifts.

If you are at all worried about going to an exercise class for health reasons, then check first with your GP. So long as you choose a class to match your capabilities, there shouldn't be a problem.

If you are doing exercises at home, to the accompaniment of a cassette for example, remember to warm up first with some loose and easy arm swinging. Stop any time the exercises hurt, or if you feel dizzy.

Some of the choices

Many adult education centres and sports centres run keep-fit classes for older people. Similarly, there may also be special sessions at your local swimming pool. You don't have to be able to swim already; there are often special classes for older non-swimmers, in which you can learn at your own pace. The library is a good source of local information. Keep an eye on local newspapers as well.

Extend (see p 145) is an organisation which specialises in classes for the older age group, consisting of music to movement. Many of the exercises are performed sitting down. If there isn't a class near you, you could order its booklet *Exercises for Senior Citizens*. Yoga is an ideal way to improve posture, breathing and suppleness. Look out for classes run by your local adult education service or contact the British Wheel of Yoga (see p 144) or the Yoga for Health Foundation (see p 146).

If you suffer aching feet, these movements will help improve circulation and muscle tone.

1 Starting from Correct Sitting Posture, imagine you are picking up sand with your toes. Curl toes underneath foot, count one; flatten foot out, count two. Do this eight times. Keeping ball of foot in contact with floor, lift toes up to ceiling and drop down, same counting as before.

2 Clasp hands over knees to keep them still and roll feet onto outer edges, curling toes in to meet in centre, count two; relax feet down, count two. Do this eight times.

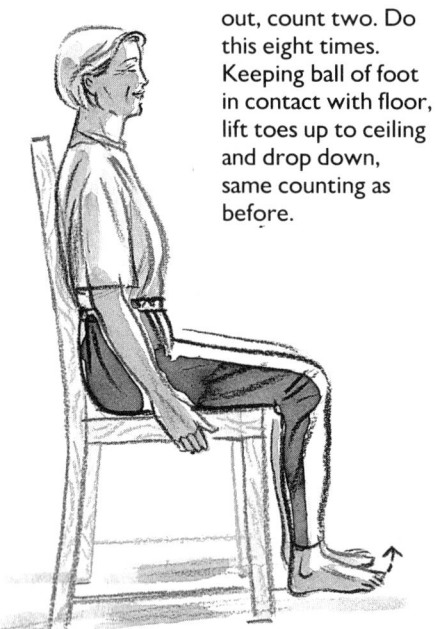

Tai Chi is growing in popularity as an activity, particularly for the older age group. Originally a martial art from China, Tai Chi, with its coordinated, choreographed movements, is now more widely used to promote positive aspects of health such as balance, breathing and body harmony.

Walking, indoor or outdoor bowling and golf are all popular activities enjoyed by many older people, either as beginners or veterans. There are also many kinds of dancing: ballroom, sequence, tap, country, folk, and Scottish. Circle dancing, which is growing in popularity, is based on folk dances from countries like Greece, Israel and the Balkans. You don't need a partner, and participation is more important than individual performance. The atmosphere is non-competitive and non-threatening; the natural physical

3 Clasp hands under right knee and straighten the leg. Point foot down, count two; push heel out, bringing foot up, count two. Do this four times and repeat with other foot.

4 Clasp hands under right knee to stabilize lower calf area, while drawing a circle with the big toe, ankle rotating. Count four each circle, and do it four times each way. Repeat with other foot.

If you suffer from tired aching feet, practising these movements will help to improve circulation and muscle tone. When walking, remember to put your heel down first and push off at the ball of the foot.

contact of holding hands in a ring can provide a healing touch for someone who is lonely or recently bereaved. The pace can be fast and frantic or slow and peaceful according to the music, which is usually taped but can be live.

The form of exercise you choose to take, and the level at which you choose to perform it, is unimportant. What matters is that you should enjoy it and look forward to it. It will help you to feel good about yourself and this will be reflected in the way you look.

Exercise machines

A wide range of home exercise equipment is sold through Argos, the catalogue-based retail outlet which offers among the most competitive prices. Leaf through the catalogue to see the kinds of things now available: treadmills, rowing machines, cycles and a variety of tortuous-looking weight sets, at a range of different prices. However, when in January 1990 *Which?* magazine tested a selection of exercise machines, available from credit card catalogues and Sunday magazines for a price of under £50, it was not impressed. Its team of experts raised the following general points.

There is a boredom factor associated with exercise machines. Many people buy machines which they rarely, if ever, use.

Exercise machines bought from a catalogue or by mail order can't be properly assessed before purchase.

People should consider the degree of fitness they are aiming for and ask themselves whether they really need an expensive machine; remember, you can improve on stamina by using an inexpensive skipping rope.

If you are keen to acquire an exercise machine, you will probably find that an exercise bike is the most useful and versatile. It would particularly suit someone living in the country, far from any kind of health or fitness centre. If you do buy a bike through mail order, make sure you can return it if it proves unsuitable, and check how long the trial period lasts. You may be lucky in finding a second-hand bargain. New or second-hand, you need to check the model carefully for stability, avoiding a machine which rocks and might upset your balance. The bike should also be adjustable so that other people can use it and so that you can measure your progress. A final suggestion is that an exercise bike might be a popular shared purchase by members of a retirement club or by residents in a block of retirement flats.

Personal freshness

There's nothing more relaxing after exercising than a hot shower or bath. You feel you have earned it. It's also vital to wash away the build-up of sweat which exercising causes – healthy in itself, but with an odour which few find attractive. Personal freshness is an important part of good grooming and has the same intangible and yet positive results; it makes us feel good about ourselves and it definitely makes us sweeter company to be with. A bubble bath may be soothing and relaxing, but a long soak in hot water won't get you any cleaner than a quick dip or a shower. In fact, wallowing in water for too long dries your skin unnecessarily. To avoid dry skin, you might replace or at least alternate bath salts or foaming bath bubbles with the use of bath oil; baby oil is cheaper and effective, although you may prefer something scented. Always rub a moisturising cream or body lotion into your skin after a bath. This kind of regular habit can transform feet, elbows and hands – all areas prone to dryness.

A shower is just as refreshing as a bath; it's also quicker and saves on water and energy. A regular bathtime session is a wonderful way to pamper yourself, and indeed, is necessary for proper skincare. Layers of rough skin tend to build up, on feet and elbows; they benefit greatly from regular friction treatment with a loofah, body brush or massage mitt. There are many products on the market, such as body scrubs and granules, which have been specially formulated to assist exfoliating – the sloughing off of layers of invisible dead skin. Rubbing with a pumice stone or handful of coarse salt will also stimulate the skin circulation. Upper arms often bear permanent goosepimples because of bad circulation, and will improve with gentle friction, followed by a spray of cold water. Be sure to rub in moisturising lotion after drying.

Personal freshness is a necessary daily habit made all the more enjoyable by the wide range of soaps and shower gels now on the market, including entire ranges designed especially for men. One last reminder on this subject; don't forget the familiar underarm deodorant. It may be small, but it's very effective!

Fragrance for all

While the need for personal freshness is a basic requirement demanded by society in general, the use of fragrance brings a greater individuality into play. It can be a subtle yet creative way of expressing yourself in public. Used with care, it is highly appreciated; everyone has enjoyed the waft of perfume or aftershave emanating from someone nearby. It is another intangible way of creating a good feeling about yourself, of enjoying the person you are.

Don't make the mistake of believing that only women should use fragrance. Fifty per cent of all men now use some form of aftershave or balm – scent by any other name. The autumn of 1990 saw the unapologetic launch of eight new fragrances for men from major fashion houses.

Advice on choosing a scent or fragrance is the same for men as it is for women. Keep it subtle. Perhaps the most elusive way to wear fragrance is by putting a few drops in the bath water.

There is only one way to choose scent and that is to try it for yourself on your own skin. The adjectives used to describe scent – such as 'woody', 'spicy', 'citrus', 'tangy' – tend to be emotive; they mean different things to different people. In addition to that, everyone's skin has an individual reaction to perfume, which affects the final result.

Guidelines for selecting a scent are as follows:

- test only one fragrance at a time, by dabbing a few drops from the tester on the inside of your wrists
- leave the shop and continue with your shopping while the warmth of your body blends with the fragrance

- breathe in the waft of scent from your wrists from time to time and you will soon know how much the fragrance appeals to you; a scent can be pleasing without it being right for you.

You may need to repeat this testing procedure a few times, but never do it more than once on the same day.

Fragrance is sold in a sensible way at branches of Body Shop. They stock a range of perfume oils which you can buy in very small quantities. This is ideal because scents tend to fade with time, particularly in centrally heated bedrooms and bathrooms. The rule is to buy little and often. Try variations on a theme, according to your mood and the season.

Feet and legs

If the way we feel is reflected in the way we look, then our feet have much to answer for. Three out of every four adults have foot problems, often as a result of wearing ill-fitting shoes in earlier days. The least you can do to make up for past neglect is to ensure that your feet are well cared for from now on. Putting up with unnecessary discomfort will interfere with your enjoyment of life and your appetite for leisure activities. Think about the future – your feet may have to last you another 30 years or so; well cared-for feet may make a big difference to getting out and about in old age. Equally, unattractive legs and feet may mar an otherwise pleasing appearance.

Hints for happy feet

For instant relief from aching and swollen feet at the end of the day, lie or sit down with your feet raised higher than your hips for about 15 minutes.

Dip tired feet alternately and for a minute at a time, in warm and then cool water. This stimulates the circulation.

When you have to stand for a period of time, take the opportunity to exercise your calf muscles. Going up on tip toe, gently raising and lowering your heels will encourage better circulation.

Always stand with your back straight, tummy and bottom tucked in and your weight evenly distributed on both feet.

Don't sit with your legs or ankles crossed for too much of the time; this restricts circulation.

When you are sitting, occasionally exercise your ankles by rotating your feet, one at a time, first in a clockwise, then an anti-clockwise direction.

At bathtime, give the hard skin areas of your feet a regular friction rub, using a loofah or massage mitt. To remove a build-up of hard skin, use a pumice stone.

Dry your feet carefully. Rub in cream every night, exercising your toes as you do so.

Consulting a chiropodist

It is advisable for corns and calluses to be treated by a professional chiropodist. Chiropodists who are state registered can use the letters SRCh after their names. You may be able to receive treatment reasonably quickly under the NHS, although this will depend on where you live and on the supply and demand of the area. There is a countrywide shortage of qualified chiropodists.

It is not necessary to have a letter of referral from a doctor in order to consult a chiropodist. Your GP or health authority can supply information about local clinics. State registered chiropodists also practise privately and can be found in the *Yellow Pages* or local *Thomson Directory*. The local NHS chiropody service may also keep a list of those registered practitioners who do private practice. Never delay getting treatment if you have a problem. Clients who are in the habit of making regular appointments for professional footcare feel this is money well spent.

Nail care

Toe nails get more difficult to cut as you get older. It's not only the business of reaching them; the nails themselves dry out and become harder to cut, even with the strongest clippers. An alternative is filing with an emery board, *running the file along the length of the nail* rather than across it. Any problems with painful or ingrowing toe nails should be taken to a chiropodist.

An excellent source of information *The Foot Care Book: An A-Z of Fitter Feet* by Judith Kemp SRCh, is published by Age Concern (see p 151).

Summer legs

Many older women feel diffident about going bare-legged in summer – yet who wants to wear stockings or tights in hot weather? Wearing cool trousers is one answer, another is to do what women did in the war when nylons were scarce – wear leg make-up. It really makes a difference to the look of a summer dress and is widely available from local chemists.

Support hosiery

Women who have spurned support hosiery as being thick and frumpy would be well-advised to take a second look. Support tights and stockings can now be ultra sheer, the equivalent of ten denier, and come in a wide range of colours including pastels, and a variety of patterns, such as rib. Some include Lycra in their composition; look out for Scholl's Lite Legs range, for example.

Support hosiery is knitted in such a way as to provide graduated support. There is greater compression at the ankle, gradually decreasing up the calf and thigh, which encourages better circulation and relieves aching legs. Support hosiery needs to be replaced regularly in order to continue its effectiveness.

Hands and nails

Well-cared-for hands always look attractive but require regular attention. They are very vulnerable to roughness and the ravages of wear and tear, and this increases with age as the skin becomes drier. A bottle of fragrance-free hand lotion kept next to the sink and the wash basin, for use every time you wash your hands, is an opportune reminder to keep up a good habit. It's a good idea to vary handcreams now and again. Some provide combined care for cuticles and nails which are ideal to use at bedtime.

Hands and nails need protection wherever possible:

- wear rubber gloves to wash up, and whenever you come into contact with water and detergent
- wear heavy-duty protective gloves and/or barrier cream for dirty jobs
- wear gloves when you go outdoors in cold weather.

Hints for happy hands

There are some gardening jobs, like taking cuttings or potting up seedlings for which gloves are too clumsy. Barrier cream is useful here. Another good tip *before* gardening is to wet your fingertips and rake them along the surface of a cake of softish toilet soap. The filling blocks out most of the soil and helps prevent grimy fingernails.

A most effective, almost magic, soap, which lifts the dirt from hands *after* gardening or dirty garage jobs is called True Grit. It contains a mixture of rosemary and pumice and is obtainable by post from Cosmetics to Go (see p 144).

As a night recovery service, petroleum jelly – Vaseline – spread thickly and generously over the hands at bedtime and allowed to soak in overnight works wonders for dry hands. You may need to wear protective cotton gloves.

A unisex manicure

Hands and nails need regular conditioning. For a thorough but quick manicure:

1 Soak the fingertips in warm soapy water to clean the nails.
2 Soak fingertips for a further five minutes in a bowl containing a couple of tablespoons of warmed almond or olive oil in order to nourish dry nails and soften hard skin.
3 Gently press back the softened cuticle with an orange stick wrapped round with cotton wool; ragged cuticles need gentle treatment.
4 Massage a little hand cream in and around each nail to encourage circulation.

Fingers, thumbs and wrists all need frequent exercising to keep them mobile. If you have arthritis in your hands, you may benefit from paraffin wax treatment. If the arthritis is severe, ask your GP about the possibility of obtaining this on the NHS from the physiotherapy department at your local hospital. Otherwise it is a standard beauty therapy treatment, obtainable from any salon.

Sun protection

A deep suntan used to provoke envy; it was a visible sign of affluence and leisure. Nowadays, while we still regard a tan as an asset, we are much more aware of how the sun can damage the skin, causing premature ageing and increasing the risk of skin cancer.

In the presence of strong sunlight, skin reacts in two ways: it activates the pigment melanin, which results in a tan, and it grows new and thicker cells to act as a barrier. The result of this can be seen in the faces of people who have spent many years out of doors in sunny climates; they have a leathery quality to their skin. The increase of certain types of skin cancer, particularly in the USA and Australia, as well as in this country, has focused attention on the importance of protecting the skin.

The Victorians were obsessive and snobbish about avoiding the sun, protecting their precious complexions with parasols and Panama hats. They carried this to extremes; even freckles were frowned on and having a tan was associated with farm workers.

It is possible today to enjoy a compromise between excessive tanning and excessive protection: a healthy glow from the fresh air and sunshine, without any of the damage. Panama hats are back in fashion, but there are other ways to care for the skin:

- reduce the time you spend in the sun and, when it is particularly hot, avoid the midday period between 11.00 am and 2.00 pm, when the sun is at its highest
- always use sunscreen products.

Sunscreen products with SPF

SPF stands for Sun Protection Factor. The measure of protection is indicated by a number ranging from 2 to 25 printed on sun care products such as lotions, creams and gels. Low numbers indicate minimum protection. Oils, for example, are only available in low and medium factors.

As yet there is no standard code for SPFs, they vary according to the manufacturer. One brand's SPF of 4 may be the equivalent of another brand's SPF of 6. For consumer guidance, branches of Boots and Body Shop provide helpful customer information by way of leaflets.

Skin needs protection after as well as before exposure to the sun. Always remember to use a complementary after-sun product or plenty of moisturiser.

Sunglasses

The sun's rays can harm the eyes as well as the skin. A good quality pair of sunglasses is essential if you spend much time in the sun. As well as all-purpose sunglasses for general use, it is now possible to buy certain types of lens which are recommended for specific uses. A polarising lens will reduce glare on water or snow; a photochromatic lens rapidly darkens as sunlight increases. As well as 'off the peg' glasses, you can have a pair made up at an optician's to your own prescription requirements. Film stars have long recognised the potential glamour of a pair of sunglasses, so choose your frames with care.

Professional services

Beauty therapy

In the past beauty salons had the reputation of being frequented primarily by rich women with time on their hands. Now the body business is one of the most important growth areas of the health and leisure industry. Clients are drawn from all classes, are of both sexes, and from all age groups.

Treatments for the face and body are available in a wide variety of different settings. Some salons are located in department stores where they are often combined with a hairdressing salon. Since space is often restricted, they tend to concentrate on facials, electrolysis and manicures. Owner-run salons often call themselves clinics or studios in order to encourage prospective male clients. Look out for the established business, which has been tried and tested, and where the owner has a recognised qualification. Health and fitness clubs now offer face and body treatments, too. Clubs which operate on a membership basis sometimes offer their facilities to non-members at off-peak times as an additional source of revenue. Finally, there are a number of beauty therapists who work from home or offer a home-visiting service.

Qualifications to look out for are indicated by the initials MBABTAC, a Member of the British Association of Beauty Therapy and Cosmetology, or IFHB, the International Federation of Health and Beauty Therapists. Anyone experiencing difficulty in finding a reputable salon should write to the Confederation of International Beauty Therapy and Cosmetology (see p144).

How to choose

Your first step when choosing professional bodycare is to call in and ask for a brochure or price list. This will indicate the range of treatments on offer as well as the cost. The brochure or price list will also give you a good impression of the credibility and character of the business. A well-run establishment with an experienced owner will offer simple explanations of the treatments on offer. It will not try to dazzle customers with pseudo-scientific jargon or make promises about unique and exciting innovations which guarantee amazing results. The best businesses offer proven treatments in a caring atmosphere, with a degree of personal and individual attention. High Street franchises advertising figure-toning with rapid inch loss are to be avoided. They fail to attract the best qualified beauty therapists.

When you have found a clinic or salon which seems satisfactory, you need to make an appointment for an initial consultation. This takes place prior to any course of treatment and is usually free. The therapist will want details of your medical history, such as varicose veins, high blood pressure or known allergies, any of which may make some treatments inadvisable.

The most popular treatments for older clients include electrolysis (for permanent facial hair removal), facials, body massage and manicure. Particularly beneficial for people with arthritis in their hands is a paraffin wax treatment, which is sometimes combined with a manicure. Steer clear of sun-tanning facilities. Skin specialists are becoming increasingly concerned about the effects on health of the use of ultra-violet sunbeds. They maintain there is now enough evidence of harmful effects on the skin to justify a recommendation that this kind of artificial tanning should be discouraged. It is certainly not recommended for older skin.

Going as a model

Beauty therapy students need models on whom they can practise the full range of treatments. The teaching environment provides you with an opportunity to experiment with quite expensive treatments, such as facials and body massage, for a nominal fee. It also offers an interesting glimpse into the professional world of beauty therapy. Students are not always school leavers; many are mature students, sometimes with a nursing background.

These kinds of courses are run by private beauty schools and colleges of further education which offer the City and Guilds Beauty Therapists Certificate Course. If you are interested in acting as a model, you should make enquiries to the course tutor in both cases. Obviously any appointment for treatment will have to fit in with the school's timetable, and you should remember that there will also be at least half a dozen other models there as well.

Aromatherapy

This therapy is particularly appropriate for older people and often suitable where body massage is not recommended. People with skin complaints, such as acne, psoriasis or eczema, can also benefit greatly from specially selected formulations.

Aromatherapy uses essential oils, stimulating or relaxing, on the face and body in order to restore a harmonious balance. Therapists work in various settings: in beauty salons, at health farms or hydros, health and fitness centres, from home or visiting clients in their own homes.

The Institute of Clinical Aromatherapy runs training courses for doctors, nurses and beauty therapists, and can supply a countrywide list of trained aromatherapists (see p 145). Prospective models for training sessions, who need to live within the South London area, should also get in touch with them.

The essential oils used in aromatherapy are highly concentrated distillations, about 100 times more powerful than in their original plant form. Essential oils, or synthetic versions, are commonly sold in High Street shops as aromatherapy products. Many have inadequate instructions concerning the necessary dilution with a carrier oil, such as sweet almond or wheatgerm, and this can be dangerous for people who use them as a perfume applied directly on the skin.

The Department of Health is under pressure to review the safety of essential oils, and the warning labels on their containers. In the meantime such oils should be used with extreme care:

- never eat or drink essential oils, or add them to food or drink
- never use them directly on the skin.

Health farms or hydros

Most people who go for a short stay on a health farm, or hydro as they are often called today, seem to enjoy the experience – so much so that they often return at a later date. Some people go to relax, others to be pampered with massage, saunas, mud baths and a wide range of beauty treatments, all in a luxurious setting. Many health hydros are well advertised in newspapers and magazines.

There is a bewildering range of treatments and facilities on offer, some included in the basic price, others as optional extras. The main criticism made by the magazine *Which?* recently was that there was little individual guidance available to help clients choose appropriate treatments. These include exercise facilities, as well as therapies such as acupuncture, osteopathy and aromatherapy. The value of single sessions of some of these therapies is highly questionable; some therapies are only beneficial as part of a long-term course of treatment. Weight reduction, for example, is dependent upon a long-term sustained programme – a quick weight loss over a few days will not achieve any lasting benefit.

Most hydros make much of their health-conscious menus; most serve light diet portions. Some will offer the option of a 48-hour lemon and water fast, others consider strict fasting to be unnecessary and undesirable.

Depending on where you live, fitness facilities and beauty treatments are probably much cheaper nearer home. Some health hydros offer savings. For example, one establishment recently introduced a Short Notice Club, offering reductions to customers able to come at the last minute or at off-peak time. If life is very stressful and you would welcome a break from home, a 2–3 day stay at a health hydro may make a wonderful change. View it as a mini-holiday with a difference.

Cosmetic surgery

Cosmetic surgery used to be the highly exclusive and expensive preserve of film stars and celebrities. Modern surgery procedures, including local anaesthetics and short overnight stays, combined with an increased demand from the public, have brought a range of cosmetic surgery treatments to more affordable levels.

Following the American trend, more older people in the UK are beginning to enquire about ways to combat the most obvious signs of ageing. Such treatments include the face lift, mini face lift, eyebag removal, eyelid improvement, the tummy tuck and the thigh lift.

Cosmetic surgery may lift those physical parts of you which need lifting, but that's all. You may be pleased with the result, but what the operation *won't* do is lift your spirits, make you less lonely or depressed, change your life or find you the perfect partner. Cosmetic surgery can't stop the clock. It can only postpone the inevitable consequences of ageing, and reputable surgeons are usually reluctant to operate on anyone whose expectations are unrealistic. Not every doctor abides by such high ethical standards. Any medical practitioner can call him or herself a cosmetic surgeon. It is important to check on the qualifications of anyone you contact. There are two reputable associations, both of which belong to the Royal College of Surgeons; they are the British Association of Plastic Surgeons (BAPS) and the British Association of Aesthetic Plastic Surgeons (BAAPS). The latter association deals solely with cosmetic work. In order to be a member of either association, you need to have been an NHS consultant for a number of years. Neither association is able to give out names of their members to the general public because this is considered to be advertising, but a GP can request this information for you.

If you already have the name and address of a possible surgeon, and wish to check whether he or she is a member, you can telephone BAPS on 071–831 5161 or BAAPS on 071–405 2234.

Collagen injections

Less drastic than cosmetic surgery, although sometimes used in conjunction with it, are collagen injections, the only method of diminishing wrinkles approved by the Department of Health.

A fine hypodermic needle is used to inject collagen into affected areas of the skin. Such injections boost the elastic effects of our own natural supply of collagen, which diminishes with time. The treatment only works on relatively superficial areas such as laughter lines or crow's-feet, and is not effective on heavy wrinkles. Its results are only temporary, lasting from three months to a year, while its costs are high. The collagen injections have to be administered by a registered physician, preferably a cosmetic surgeon, who will perform a skin test to check against allergic reaction.

Body care: a final thought

Men and women whose appearance is very much part of their professional image devote both time and money to keeping trim and up-to-date with their looks. They work at it not only because it's bread and butter, but because they appreciate the spin-off – the way it makes them feel, and the tremendous effect on everyone they come into contact with.

However busy we are, we should all allocate some energy and effort towards improving our outward selves. It's so easy not to bother and to sink into a retirement routine which is not very stimulating. One of the best tonics for face and figure is, of course, a holiday. Invariably, people come back from holiday looking better, fitter and younger. Remember the comment of film star Gloria Swanson who, when looking at her passport photo, made the remark: 'If I look like this, I need the trip!'

Skin & Face Care

THERE IS A GREAT DIFFERENCE BETWEEN PAINTING A FACE AND NOT WASHING IT

Thomas Fuller

■

The quality of your skin in your 50s and upwards will largely depend on how well it's been treated in the past; but there are other factors, too. People with oily skins tend to develop fewer wrinkles as they get older; smokers develop more. The skin of anyone who has lived in a sunny climate or worked outdoors will most likely have developed a tanned and leathery look. If you tend to be on the plump side, your face may show fewer signs of ageing.

Most skins, however, suffer from neglect and this is something that can be remedied by means of a regular skincare routine. Both men and women need to safeguard against dryness, particularly with older skin. Washing with a vegetable-based soap will help. Moisturisers will also keep the skin supple.

It's a widely recognised and researched fact that in spite of several ranges of skin care products available for men, they still make surreptitious use of their partner's skin products. Some protective lotions and hand creams are consequently now labelled as being for general family use. The regular use of moisturiser, not only at night but also as a protection against harsh weather, is particularly recommended for men. Prevention against dryness is preferable to treatment afterwards, whether the cause is winter weather or summer sun. Lips are particularly vulnerable: lip salve provides winter protection while its summer equivalent has an added sunscreen.

Female face care

Whether you use make-up or not, face and neck cleansing night and morning should be a regular habit, if not a ritual. This will keep your skin clear and healthy, as well as keeping it supple. Cleansing alone isn't enough; for the complete routine you should cleanse, tone and moisturise. The different parts of the routine require different products. A question many people will want to ask is what's wrong with soap and water? The answer is that it doesn't remove make-up and it can make the skin feel taut and dry after washing, due to the alkaline content used to neutralise the animal fat from which most soap is made. (A vegetable-based soap is kinder to your skin.)

If you really are wedded to the idea of using a bar of something, then search out one of the solidified cleansing bars on the market. They are used like soap, but have a creamier content.

Don't stint on skincare. With a good quality product, a little goes a long way. In fact, if you use too much, you only overload the skin, and the extra is wasted. Own-name brands from Sainsbury's, Boots and Marks and Spencer are all good value for money.

Cleansing

There is a wide choice available, including creams, lotions, milk, gels and mousse. You need something which suits your skin but which you enjoy using and find easy and convenient. Otherwise you will begin to skip the routine. As most older skins tend towards dryness, your best choice may well be a cream. Ensure that this isn't too heavy and doesn't drag your skin when removed with damp cotton wool.

It's fun to try different products and alternate them from time to time, as well as using something different night and morning. If, for example, you do wear make-up, you could use cream remover at night, and a lighter creamy type lotion for the quick morning cleanse, more to soften the skin than anything else.

Do use a special remover if you wear eye make-up, since face cleansers are usually too rich and heavy. There are many brands available. Remember that the skin around the eyes is particularly delicate, so don't stretch it unduly. Eye gel gives a refreshing cool lift to tired and droopy eyelids; a couple of cucumber slices or even cold tea bags, held over closed eyelids for a few moments act in the same way.

Treating yourself to a face mask every couple of weeks will cleanse and liven up the complexion and give your face a glow. For a dry skin, choose a mask with a moisturising cream rather than a clay base. Many masks have a fruit, vegetable or herb content as well.

Toning

The purpose of a toner, or skin freshener, is to remove all traces of greasy cleanser. If you've used a wash-off cleanser, such as a mousse, the water will have already done this job. Avoid toners which contain alcohol, since these dry the skin. A good substitute for toner or skin freshener is mineral water.

Nourishing

A tiny dollop of a good night cream, gently massaged into the skin of face and neck will be quickly absorbed. The last thing anyone wants is a thick greasy layer. You can buy special lightweight cream for around the eye area. If by any chance you buy a night cream which is too heavy for your liking, just use it on another part of the body – elbows or feet, perhaps – and remember not to buy it again. Beware of false claims certain manufacturers make about their products; nobody has yet invented the antidote to natural ageing.

Packaging

Often our choice of a product is influenced as much by its packaging as by its contents. Think about your needs and your budget before selecting a giant-size glass container. Remember that some of the more expensive brands are deceptively packaged; an inner container holds far less than the outward appearance of the pack indicates.

For people who travel a lot, or go to stay with friends and relatives on a regular basis, glass jars and bottles which are heavy and breakable can be a nuisance. Of course you could decant any liquid contents into a small plastic container but why not choose this kind of packaging in the first place?

Trial sizes are popular with older customers whose finances aren't always able to cope with large expensive purchases. Cyclax is a reputable brand which favours small containers, and is widely available.

Body Shop has a positive approach to packaging. Its products are sold in simple plastic containers bearing informative labels. Customers get a reduction on most products when they return the original container for a refill.

Skincare by post

A number of small mail order firms supply good quality skincare products, including oils, shampoos and make-up, through the post. Brochure descriptions are informative; a telephone ordering service is available; deliveries are generally prompt, and staff are happy to answer queries over the telephone. While this is an especially convenient service for those who live far from shops, everyone can benefit from good quality products not otherwise available through normal retailers.

Cosmetics to Go (see p 144) is a company whose products make ideal presents mainly because of their original presentation and packaging. They sell skincare items designed for extremities of climate from frost and windproof protection for skiing to sun protection products for safaris. Their vegetable soap – True Grit – containing rosemary and pumice, is ideal for use after gardening or garage work. Their fruit face masks – made from asparagus, herb and lemon – are freshly made; customers are advised to keep them in the fridge and their shelf life is only 17 days. Should you live in or visit the Poole area, you can actually watch them being mixed.

Martha Hill (see p 146) sells skincare items, shampoos and perfume oils as well as a men's range called David Hill. Trial sizes are available and containers are returnable.

SFL (see p 146) is a company which is well-known throughout staff associations for the offers it promotes to employees. Before retiring, you may well have enjoyed the benefits of buying 'famous name' cosmetics and fragrances at discount prices. You still can, by writing for their current leaflet.

Facial hair

Facial hair can be a problem for both men and women. Taking some care with it is part of good grooming. Men who have thick and bushy eyebrows which meet in the middle often look quite fierce, at least to the unsuspecting stranger. Some judicious trimming, and the use of tweezers to pluck the offending hairs from the bridge of the nose could help to create a more favourable first impression. Hairy nostrils also need frequent attention. Simply snip the longest hairs with a pair of sharp nail scissors.

Women who have dark hairs growing on their upper lip can bleach them at home using a product such as Jolen, which is widely available. A more permanent treatment is removal by electrolysis but this should only be carried out by a professionally trained beautician (see p 90). Waxing is another depilatory treatment, but the results are not permanent.

Face exercises

Some people swear by face exercise as a means of keeping wrinkles at bay. Regularly exercising of the face and neck strengthens supporting muscles and discourages lines from forming. The exercises contained in a recent publication; *Eva Fraser's Facial Workout,* are also available on video (see p 147).

Face exercises can be usefully combined with the following speech exercise routine, valuable practice for anyone who has to speak in public.

1. Face a mirror.
2. Say loudly but slowly the following series of vowel sounds: oo, oh, aw, ah, ay, ee.
3. Enunciate clearly, and vary the voice – going up and down the scale alternately.
4. Greatly exaggerate the lip movements involved so that you get the

purest vowel sound, combined with maximum mobility of the mouth muscles.

Dental care

Fresh breath and well-maintained teeth and dentures are essential if you are to present a well-groomed and pleasing appearance. Regular mouth care involves looking after the gums as well as the teeth. It means brushing the teeth every day, and that includes dentures or partial dentures. The use of dental floss to remove debris from between the teeth can be helpful, as can the occasional use of soluble disclosing tablets, obtainable from chemists. Dissolved in water and washed round the mouth, these pink tablets show up the areas where plaque has not been adequately removed – a useful check.

Regular visits to the dentist are important for everyone, including denture wearers, who require a good and comfortable fit. A poor fit encourages a 'nutcracker-jaw' look (think of Les Dawson's female impersonations), which is caused by the muscles of the lower jaw working overtime to hold dentures in place. Dentures need relining from time to time; they may also need replacing.

NHS or private?

Changes to the system of NHS dental care introduced in October 1990 mean that you can now register with a NHS dentist for a 'continuing care' contract. You will be offered an overall treatment plan which may include suggestions for some private treatment. Private treatment is entirely optional. The estimated costs of your treatment plan will be itemised. The patient is required to pay a percentage of any NHS treatment to a maximum figure for any single course of treatment. The costs of private treatment must be met by the patient in full. This new contract entitles you to emergency cover arrangements. Unless you are registered with a dentist, it may prove difficult to get emergency treatment – for example, repairs to dentures.

Dentists in group practices will be providing patients with information leaflets, outlining their particular services, such as a hygienist who undertakes routine cleaning and gives advice on the correct brushing of the teeth and care of the gums. In the meantime the new arrangements are explained in various leaflets: *A change in dental care for you* and *How things are changing at the dentist's,* obtainable from the British Dental Association on receipt of a stamped addressed envelope (see p 144).

Finding a new dentist

The best recommendation is that of friends or well-trusted acquaintances. In the absence of this, contact your local Family Health Services Authority (formerly called the Family Practitioners Committee). Their lists now give fuller information about NHS dentists and their services, but do not include dentists who are exclusively private.

Don't be afraid of your dentist

Many people are too nervous to visit their dentist on a regular basis. Only when they are in extreme pain will they actually make an appointment. This fear can often be traced back to a bad experience at the dentist's in childhood or long ago, something which shouldn't happen today with modern techniques. Another improvement is the reduction in the time required for dental appointments. Quick-acting painkilling injections, and changes in the technology, mean that patients may be in and out of the surgery within 20 minutes.

Dental phobia, which is more widespread than most people imagine, is now recognised by dentists and there are special techniques to help patients cope with it. These are explained in a leaflet *Don't be afraid,* obtainable from the British Dental Health Foundation (see p 144). Other leaflets include *Dental care for older people* and *Your guide to dentures.* Full information concerning NHS dental treatment is obtainable from the Information Department at Age Concern England. Please enclose a 9" x 6" self-addressed envelope.

Make-up

Old habits die hard

Many women wear make-up for no other reason than because they have always done so. They almost feel obliged to wear it. Some say they feel 'undressed' without it and wouldn't dream of confronting the outside world in such a state.

There are women who wear precisely the same make-up during spring, summer, autumn and winter, for shopping, for the office, even for a keep-fit class. Make-up used in this way is often a cover-up mask, literally as well as figuratively, and does little to enhance the appearance of an individual's face.

Reluctant users

A different group are those women who decline to wear make-up for reasons which may have little to do with their own personal choice or preference. A few years ago, fanatical feminists scorned the use of make-up as an artificial means of enhancement, worn by women to attract men. By using it, women were effectively falling into the trap laid for them by men, casting themselves in the role of attractive nonentities whose lives were dedicated to giving pleasure – to men.

Other women were brought up by strict parents who associated the wearing of make-up with sinful, 'scarlet' women. Such women were often brought up to be unassertive and conformist and have found these early influences extremely inhibiting.

Enhancing your appearance doesn't mean you have an ulterior motive or that you are a sexual predator. Whether or not you wear make-up, how much and how often, is a personal decision. It's a conscious and variable choice, like which clothes to wear, and is based on the occasion, the time of day, the season, and your own mood. Make-up isn't compulsory, neither is it a form of permanent camouflage. It's a means of enhancement as and when you want to use it. When assessing your make-up, always ask the question: 'What I am trying to achieve?'.

▲ Colourful checks stave off drabness and complement easy-fit pleat top trousers or jeans for any age group.

▶ Relaxed, easy-fit cotton 'chinos' are second nature to the young, yet they're also ideal for maturer builds. Colourful shirts suggest a youthful spirit, whereas a bland look is monotonous at any age.

◀ Most of what's good for the young is also good for older people, even if they style it differently. This blouson top is a case in point.

▼ Replace a mini or leggings with a classic shirt and skirt and you find that you too can wear a big bold sweater. Go for a loose long line for maximum flattery.

▲ The grey business suit is curiously ageing.

▶ Suits that can be formal but in lighter-hearted shades make an upbeat impression. Colour Analysts are trained to pinpoint the colours that work best for each client.

Updating your make-up

Many older women could make more of their looks than they presently do. Often it's not their clothes but their make-up which lets them down. Make-up, like hairstyles, can easily get stuck in a time warp unless you make the effort to keep up to date with new products and techniques. Less make-up, not more, is often the message for an older skin; but it needs to be carefully selected and cleverly applied.

Don't think of yourself as a lost cause. There are many opportunities to obtain professional, practical help in updating, choosing and applying make-up (see p 111). You might start by looking at books on the subject. Some are by make-up artists as well-known as Barbara Daly, and these you can borrow from the library. *The Clothes Show* and other television programmes sometimes feature items on make-up, and often include an older woman among the demonstration models.

Foundation cream

A foundation cream is probably the most problematic cosmetic for older women. It shouldn't leave your face looking heavily made up or a different colour; it should have the lightest possible texture. Have you ever noticed, perhaps when hospital visiting, how much more attractive and youthful some women look without their regular make-up? Too much dark foundation actually draws attention to an older skin because it looks false and unharmonised.

As you get older, your skin tone fades; it is essential to choose a foundation as close as possible to your natural skin tone.

When testing a new foundation, forget all about the dab on the inside of the wrist. The best test area is under the side of the chin, which is marginally lighter than the cheek area. Check there isn't an obvious dark patch; the foundation should almost disappear.

Two foundations can always be blended and mixed to get a better skin match, but they must be the same brand. Some foundations are oil-based; others water-based.

Not everyone needs a foundation cream. Its purpose is to even out the complexion. Some women use it only in the winter months, but not in the summer when the face has a natural glow from fresh air and a moderate amount of sun. Women with an older, lined skin may prefer to use foundation only on the cheeks in order to even up the skin tones. A concealer, a foundation cream in concentrated form, may be more appropriate in covering red thread veins on the cheeks and to disguise liver spots and other small discolourations. Liver spots, brown patches which appear most frequently on the hands and face, can be removed professionally by a beauty therapist using chemical peeling or freezing with liquid nitrogen. Treatment is also possible for broken veins. For information about other skin blemishes see page 138.

The following tips are worth noting when applying foundation cream.

Always use a moisturiser before applying foundation. Allow it to soak in well for at least ten minutes if you have the time.

Apply foundation sparingly, using a small dampened sponge rather than fingers. Make sure you blend it in well around the jaw line.

Take special care around the hair-line and eyebrows. The reverse side of the dampened sponge can be used to remove excess foundation.

If your foundation clogs and collects in the wrinkles, then you probably need to pay more attention to your skin care routine to soften the skin. You should also use one of the water-based foundations and apply it quite thinly with your sponge.

Basic make-up equipment

Your most important prop is a well placed, well lit mirror with a good source of both natural and artificial light. If you wear glasses, then a pair of 'half specs' are useful when tidying up eyebrows.

In addition you will need:

- a magnifying mirror for close inspection
- small sponges, synthetic rather than real, but as firm and dense as possible
- a velour powder puff for gently pressing on loose translucent powder. Don't overdo this or it will settle in the creases
- brushes of varying sizes; one the size of a man's shaving brush is ideal for dusting off surplus powder; smaller ones are used to apply blusher

and eye make-up. If you want to be really professional, use a lip brush to outline the lips before applying lipstick. An alternative is a lip pencil.

Sponges and brushes can almost always be bought locally. Free advice leaflets are often available as well as information about products.

Barbara Daly's Colouring range, at the Body Shop is reasonably priced and aims to be eminently usable by the average woman and to replace mystique with shared technique, that is, the user learning the skills for herself (see sketches on p 72).

Make-up lessons

The mystique about make-up has been deliberately sponsored by the big cosmetic houses. A great critic of this is Joan Price, a former beauty editor, whose response was to open The Face Place in Chelsea in the 1960s. She saw that many women were put off asking for advice about make-up in department stores because of the insensitive approach of cosmetic consultants, only interested in selling their own brand. By contrast, The Face Place pioneered make-up lessons where women of all ages could update their know-how as well as getting objective advice on a range of brands.

Since the 1960s, The Face Place has developed and expanded its services, and now provides a range of salon treatments for face and body. They still give over 8,000 make-up lessons a year. As well as offering impartial advice on different brands, they also stock products from over 18 leading cosmetic houses, ranging from the inexpensive houses like Mary Quant, Innoxa and Almay to the pricier ones like Estée Lauder, Christian Dior and Lancôme.

Lunchtime group sessions have an informal atmosphere and customers living in or visiting London can try out and compare products, receiving as little or as much professional help as they require. These group sessions of 10–12 people take place from 11.30 am to 2.30 pm and include a light lunch. You might also find some of the tips on how to use make-up given on page **104** helpful if you don't feel very confident about your current approach.

Try before you buy

Many of the companies which offer colour analysis sessions for women (see p 27) also offer a combined make-up demonstration, using the company's own cosmetics, which are invariably of high quality. This offers you the opportunity to try a foundation which matches your individual skin tone. Since a good foundation match makes so much difference to the enhancement of an older skin, it's probably a good idea to buy the recommended foundation there and then.

You may feel rather wary about the consultant's suggestions regarding eye make-up and lipstick, particularly if this is a cautious area for you. Be open minded; you may be pleasantly surprised at the result, although it may take some getting used to. Colour analysis aims to encourage women of all ages to use colour more adventurously, and a trained analyst will provide sound guidance. Cosmetics which are specially chosen to blend in with your skin pigmentation shouldn't look garish.

At the end of the session you will be given a list of recommended items, including blushers, eye shadows and lipsticks, all selected to coordinate with your natural colouring. There is an after-sales service for future purchases but no undue sales pressure.

Home shopping

Choosing make-up in your own or a neighbour's home can be a comfortable and convenient option, provided you don't feel pressurised to buy. The best known doorstep selling company is Avon, who now code every item as being suitable either for warm skin tones (peach or yellow) or cool skin tones (pink). An additional safeguard is the company policy of a full refund if the customer is not satisfied. Your local representative will, if requested, show you a video called *Beauty at your Fingertips*. If you want to get in touch with your local Avon representative, the address and telephone number of the head office is on page 143.

Party plan classes

Jafra Cosmetics International (see p 145), a subsidiary of Gillette Industries

Ltd, is another company selling its products in a domestic setting. It holds classes, led by a company-trained consultant, in the home of a hostess. This is a party plan arrangement whereby the hostess receives a free gift.

The class is based on one of three topics: skincare, body care or make-up. In a skincare class, the consultant will assess your skin's humidity with an electronic programmer and you can then try the recommended cleanser, skin freshener, moisturiser and face mask.

A body care session includes either a manicure or pedicure featuring an almond oil peel to soften the skin. While hands or feet are soaking, the consultant demonstrates the rest of the body care product range which includes shampoos and fragrances.

Those taking part in a make-up class complete a colour profile chart, enabling the consultant to advise on their best colours. You can then try out eye make-up, blushers and lipsticks from a wide range.

Inner and outer beauty

For every older woman who is actively enjoying the freedom of middle age, pursuing new interests or careers, developing latent talents and generally making up for lost time, there are probably several others who feel that life has very little left to offer besides increasing emptiness and loneliness.

Bereavement, divorce, family rifts, redundancy – these are all negative experiences which some survive more successfully than others. There are people who get more than their fair share of misfortune, leaving an underlying sense of bitterness and recrimination which is not always openly recognised.

Many women have spent much of their lives catering for the demands of home and family, often at the expense of their own personal growth and development. Again, there may be undercurrents of martyrdom and sourness which divert energy, stunt initiative and deny peace of mind.

Counselling, psychotherapy and assertiveness courses are all possible rescue services, but these growth experiences are not usually directed at the older age group. Moreover, people who already lack conviction and confidence in themselves are seldom able to take such positive action.

Beauty therapy can have a healing role here. Not everyone, particularly women on their own, can afford regular treatments in a professional salon. However, there are many alternatives which can provide an occasional enjoyable psychological 'lift'. Woman can be a great help and support to each other – sisters under the skin in fact. Any encouragement we can give to an unhappy older woman which revives an interest in her appearance is a positive gesture. Looking better can be the first step to feeling better about life.

A ministry of beauty

Jean Guthrie Beauty Care is a Christian movement which began ten years ago in South Africa. The company was set up when Jean Guthrie, who had been in the beauty business in Johannesburg for some years, became a committed Christian and felt she should use her work to bring the message of inner and outer beauty to women everywhere.

Her skincare product range is sold direct to the public rather than through retail outlets. Trained consultants working in teams offer free mini-facials and beauty clinics as well as inner and outer beauty talks. Meetings usually begin with prayers.

Helen Weir, Jean Guthrie's sister, who has been involved with the business in the UK for the past four years, explains their two-fold aim: 'There's a product and there's a ministry. We combine the two and mould them to people's needs.'

Helen gives talks to church-based groups, in which she discusses the built-in resistance some religious-minded people have to the very idea of beauty care, which has been associated with vanity and wickedness. Her movement is small but growing, and there are consultants in different parts of the country. The company is an Associate Member of the Institute of Health and Beauty Therapists. For further information on Jean Guthrie Beauty Care, write to the address on page 145.

Growing older gracefully

Those people who have achieved harmony and peace with themselves and the world are probably the ones best able to grow old with grace and dignity. This positive attitude reveals itself both in their relationships and in the pride they have in their appearance, which continues well into old age. There are others, however, whose self-image is badly denied. They dread being seen as fading flowers or has-beens. It's often said that men or women who have been exceptionally attractive in younger days feel the loss of their looks more acutely than more ordinary-looking folk, almost like a bereavement. People who have always equated their physical attractiveness with a feeling of success can feel bereft without this prop. Often, these are people who have failed to develop alternative facets to their lives – other talents and interests or the social skills needed to relate to others in a non-competitive way. The loss of looks may be accompanied by a loss of self-esteem and confidence which can affect the ability to make new friends.

Such people will try anything in the vain attempt to stop the clock: garishly dyeing their hair, wearing heavy make-up, resorting to cosmetic surgery. All too frequently this exacerbates the problem and they look worse as a result. Ironically, these are the very people whom reputable cosmetic surgeons will counsel against surgery for the very reason that surgery can only postpone, not prevent, the inevitable effects of ageing.

Anti-ageing products: false claims

Some people are very susceptible to advertisements for expensive skin products which promise to revitalise and regenerate the appearance. These advertisements are deliberately aimed at the older age group and emphasise the most unpleasant aspects of an ageing appearance: crow's-feet, wrinkles, sagging skin and so on. Many appear in the colour supplements to serious newspapers, perhaps as Direct Reader Offers, which gives them a credibility they don't deserve. Typical promises are: 'Within days you will look younger'; 'Put the brakes on the ageing process'; 'You have 100 days to grow youthful skin and look years younger'. Such promises, accompanied by before and after photographs, carry glowing endorsements from existing users. They are also 'backed' by pseudo-scientific claims which may have little basis in reality.

Two skincare companies in the USA declared their product 'carries anti-ageing agents into the skin's cellular structure' and 'reconstructs the deepest epidermal layers of the vulnerable skin around your eyes'. In the United States, however, the consumer enjoys a far greater protection than here. These two claims were retracted by the cosmetic manufacturers after pressure from the US Food and Drugs Administration. In the UK we can only complain to the Advertising Standards Authority.

In the USA cosmetic ingredient labelling is obligatory, unlike here. While the main advantage of cosmetic ingredient labelling is to assist in the diagnosis and treatment of allergies (see p 137) it would have other benefits. Such a step would begin to curb advertising excesses, since the listing of ingredients gives alert consumers a basis for comparison between different brands.

In the absence of such consumer protection, the false and misleading advertisements which prey upon the older individual's fear of ageing are not going unnoticed. Organisations such as the British Association of Dermatologists, whose members are medical specialists in skin care, as well as Age Concern England on behalf of the older generation, actively monitor and lobby against this dishonest advertising. If you, as an individual, feel equally strongly, there is still room for your own complaint.

If you see an advertisement which gives incorrect or misleading information, complain to the Advertising Standards Authority (see the address on p 143). Name the company whose product was advertised, the paper or magazine in which the advertisement appeared, and the date. It is obviously helpful to enclose a copy or photocopy of the advertisement if you can. Explain in detail what you feel is wrong with the advertisement.

By taking this kind of positive action you are not only protecting gullible individuals from parting with their money, but also helping to change society's prejudice that growing older is a miserable and negative experience.

HAIR CARE

THERE'S ONE THING ABOUT BALDNESS – IT'S NEAT

Don Herold

■

Whatever your age, the condition of your hair reflects the state of your general health, and vice versa. A well-balanced diet with lots of fresh fruit and vegetables, adequate protein and plenty of drinking water is important, not only for healthy hair but for overall fitness as well.

If your hair is not in a healthy state, and this isn't due to overperming or a similar cause, then check on the condition of your nails as well. Hair and nails are a useful barometer for measuring health. Nails, like hair, are a form of protein, and any deficiency in vitamins or minerals will show in brittleness and splitting. If this is the case, then a visit to your GP to discuss your diet may be called for. Smoking, alcohol and drugs can also affect the condition of your hair adversely.

Day-to-day hair care

In days gone by, it was customary for hair to be brushed vigorously and regularly but to be washed quite rarely. There were also strange taboos with quasi-religious origins about women and girls not washing their hair during a period. These habits of obsessive brushing and infrequent washing were based on fallacies rather than facts about hair structure. There was some common sense involved however. Soap was much harsher than the scientifically-researched shampoos of today, while brushes made from natural bristle were much kinder to the hair than their modern plastic equivalents.

The rules for hair care are now very different. It may be difficult to distinguish fiction from fact in the advertisements for hair products from rival companies. The following advice is based on unbiased information from the Institute of Trichologists (see p 120), whose qualified practitioners specialise in disorders of the hair and scalp.

Brushing

Brushing the hair is of no particular health benefit. In fact it may cause damage and can over-stimulate the sebaceous glands which make the hair greasy.

If you do use a brush, then choose one which is made of natural bristle with wide spacing, rather than one made of nylon or plastic.

Washing

Frequent washing will not affect the hair; oily hair will not become oilier; dry hair will not become drier.

Use only a little of a mild shampoo, and keep the water on the cool side. You need shampoo your hair only once if you wash it frequently.

Even when you have found a shampoo which suits your hair, alternate this with another product from time to time. Shampoos contain different ingredients and hair is very individual.

Always rinse the hair well when you wash it, preferably a couple of times. A final cold rinse will help to make the hair shinier, as will a couple of drops of lemon juice or vinegar.

Conditioning

A conditioner may help if the hair is dull or brittle or lacking in body. Treatment conditioners are best bought from a hairdresser who can advise on the most appropriate product for your hair.

For an over-the-counter general purpose conditioner, shop around for a product which suits your hair. As with shampoos, switch products from time to time as they all contain different ingredients.

Conditioners are for the hair, not the scalp. So consider your hair as a fabric and concentrate on the hair, particularly the ends.

Conditioners coat the outside of the hair, and they work fast. Keeping them on longer than two or three minutes is not necessary.

Remember to rinse well after applying the conditioner.

Protecting your hair

One of the principal properties of hair is its elasticity, particularly when it is wet. However, the hair's ability to stretch without breaking is greatly reduced by chemical processes and by the ultra-violet rays in sunshine. Both can cause havoc by dehydrating hair, making it break and split.

Prevention is always better than cure, so be aware of the following risks, and take the suggested precautions.

Over-exposure to the sun:

- wear a wide-brimmed hat or scarf, especially during the hottest part of the day
- use a sun protection barrier cream if you have a bald patch.

After-effects of swimming:

- always rinse the hair in fresh water after swimming in the sea or in pools
- wear a cap for additional protection.

Styling methods using heat:

- avoid the frequent use of hot dryers, particularly blow dryers held close to the hair
- avoid the over-use of heated rollers and heated curling tongs which can dry and split the hair.

Overprocessing:

- avoid too frequent perms, bleaching and colouring, allowing a period of at least a fortnight between perming and colouring

- streaking, hi-lights and lo-lights are kinder to the hair than all-over permanent colouring and also avoid the problem of re-touching the roots as the hair grows
- ask your hairdresser whether your hair colour treatment could be of the semi-permanent, vegetable kind; these don't affect the structure of the hair, they merely coat it.

Problem solving

Damaged hair

There is a successful home treatment for hair which has been damaged by the natural wear and tear of a holiday. Gently rub warmed olive oil into your hair and scalp, wrap your head in a warm towel and allow the oil to soak in for a few hours before shampooing.

Professional treatments for damaged hair are available at hairdressers. A hairdresser who is familiar with your hair may advise on the most appropriate product for home or salon use. Alternatively, you may wish for a more objective professional opinion, especially if the damage has been caused by overprocessing at the hairdresser's in the first place.

A trichologist, whose training overlaps the medical and the cosmetic aspects, can deal with hair texture problems as well as disorders of the scalp such as persistent dandruff. Members of the Institute of Trichologists can be recognised in the *Yellow Pages* by the initials AIT (Associate) or MIT (Member) after their name. A list of countrywide, qualified, registered practitioners can be obtained by sending a stamped addressed envelope to the Institute at the address on page 145.

Dandruff

The flaking-off of dry skin cells, commonly referred to as dandruff, can be a short-term nuisance. One cause is the residue of shampoo or hair spray. A medicated shampoo may solve the problem, but is not very gentle and should not be used too frequently, especially on permed or coloured hair. Milder shampoos are sold in health shops; results may be slower but they are kinder to both hair and scalp. Another cause of dandruff is an allergy to certain foods, in which case some modification of diet may be called for. If the problem persists, professional advice should be sought.

Which hairdresser?

Hair is the one aspect of our appearance over which we have least control. Looking after hair is a perpetual compromise between maintaining it in a naturally healthy state and preventing damage through over-treatment. While we can all benefit from the improving skills of the hairdresser, too much intervention by way of perms and colouring will detract from our appearance.

Finding and sticking to a hairdresser you can trust is important for the following reasons.

Only by going back to the same hairdresser will you give him or her the chance to learn about your hair and how it reacts. However skilled and experienced a hairdresser may be, hair is an individual fibre with a life of its own.

A one off hairdresser will only be interested in the short-term result of a single visit, whereas a regular hairdresser has the responsibility for long-term care.

Your own hairdresser is more likely to give advice on suitable products and show you how to look after your hair in between salon visits.

Men as well as women often remain loyal to a tried and trusted barber or hairdresser. No one likes the uncertainty of finding someone new. However, there are times when a change is necessary and desirable. You may feel you'd like to go somewhere a little more stylish; that your present hairdresser's perception of you has become limited. In addition, men are sometimes faced with a big decision – whether or not to go unisex.

Going unisex

Many older men still prefer to visit the traditional barber's shop where they can always be sure of getting what they (and an army sergeant) call a good haircut. Technically there's nothing wrong with the cutting – it's just that there's too much of it. These skilled barbers tend to give customers their money's worth, to the last half millimetre. Even men fortunate enough to have a thick head of hair with a natural wave may emerge like shorn sheep.

A good haircut should be flattering and enhance a man's appearance. True, men don't have all the options that some women have when it comes to choosing a hairstyle, but the length, the placing of a parting, how the hair lies around the ears and shapes into the nape of the neck, whether to have sideburns or not, where the fullness needs to be – all these details add up and make an enormous difference to the whole appearance. You can really see the full effect only if the hair is washed and styled as well as cut.

There are barbers who shampoo and style as well as cut, of course, but they tend to be in cities, and are not always easily accessible. The alternative to the dry-cut barber is usually a unisex salon, which can send the average older man into a panic. So, what are the usual male excuses for not going to a unisex hairdresser?

> **'M**en cut better than women'. A lot of people would (and would not) agree. Anyway, there are plenty of male stylists in unisex salons. Many small salons are run by Italian or Spanish owners who originally trained as barbers.
>
> **'T**he barber is so much cheaper. Salons are expensive'. Since when was it worth paying someone to spoil your whole appearance? Why pay for a good quality suit, shirt and tie and end up looking as if you've just emerged from a WW2 prison camp?

Perhaps it's not fair to put all the blame on the dry-cut barber, who is only providing the service he thinks the customer wants. Perhaps it's the customer who should have a rethink and be a little more positive about the end result. What is wrong with wanting to look your best? If the truth were told, what embarrasses many older men about unisex salons is the ambience of what they see as a ladies-only preserve – the pink parlour syndrome. Look around: there is no shortage of unisex salons. They are quite common in every High Street, in department stores and also in health and leisure centres. Look at the design, the décor, the services on offer, the stylists and the clientele. There is bound to be one to suit you.

Finding a new hairdresser

The range of hairdressers available will depend on where you live, what facilities are at hand, the availability of transport and the distance you are prepared to travel.

The following are some guidelines to get you started.

Try and act on the personal recommendation of a contemporary. If you like the way an acquaintance or friend has had their hair done, don't be shy in asking them which hairdresser they use.

The *Yellow Pages* or *Thomson Directory* will give a list of addresses and telephone numbers of local hairdressers. You may like to take a look at the outside of the actual salon before making an appointment. Parking may be a practical consideration.

You may prefer to get the feel of a place first by booking a shampoo and finish, before committing yourself to anything more expensive.

When you do come to make a first appointment at a new salon, make a point of asking for the most experienced stylist/colourist. Otherwise you might get stuck with the most inexperienced staff member for every subsequent visit.

The department store salon

Older shoppers are known to prefer shopping in department stores. Stores used to run their own hairdressing departments, but now the trend is for these to be specialist salons run by hairdressing chains. Glemby, one of the biggest, have 90 salons in stores such as Owen Owen, House of Fraser, BHS and Lewis's, as well as 33 salons in Asda Superstores. These are all unisex salons and many combine hairdressing with a range of beauty treatments.

The advantage of these salons is that you are more or less assured of a certain standard (these chains usually run their own training programmes), and they do cater for older customers. This, of course, is only an advantage to those who prefer the safe and sure: it can be a disadvantage to anyone trying to avoid a typecast look.

Where not to go again

Any woman over 50 will recall the time when a session at the hairdresser's took place in the privacy of a separate individual cubicle. This may seem ludicrous today but it did ensure that the customer got the undivided attention of her hairdresser.

Older customers today frequently criticise the annoying habit of younger hairdressers carrying on a conversation – over the client's head – with the stylist who is working alongside. It is usually in the smaller owner-run salons that this takes place. Possibly, young staff don't see this as rudeness, but older people do find this behaviour offensive and should perhaps voice their objections at the time.

As a service industry increasingly dependent on older customers, hairdressers should place a high priority on good manners and communication skills. This needs to be emphasised throughout a young trainee's apprenticeship or college diploma course.

The need for better communication

Hairdressers are notorious for making assumptions about what older customers want. Older customers, which usually means anyone over the age of 40, are seen as unadventurous, stick-in-the-mud and unwilling to try anything new.

'They complain that today's perms don't last like they used to; but then neither do they damage the hair the way they used to', was the comment of one hairdresser. This says as much about poor communication skills as a lack of creativity. Few seem able to talk about new products and their purpose effectively. While most older ladies probably do not seek extremes in style, it is hard to believe that so many of them would really choose the rigid, static, wig-like look of the once-a-week shampoo and set compared to the loose, casual, easy-to-manage, look of today, made possible by mousses and gels. College courses should be more aware of the need to bridge generation gaps in customer relations.

Discounts for senior citizens

With cheap rates for senior citizens, you get what you pay for, most likely the typical, soft, all-over curly perm from a shop generating business on its quiet days. You will be stereotyped as an 'OAP', not as an individual with your own tastes and preferences.

It is far better to go to a more up-market salon, many of which advertise 'early bird' appointments. These offer reduced rates to customers of any age group who can make appointments at off-peak times such as between 9.00 am and 11.00 am, or on particular days early in the week. Another system of price reduction is called 'standby', like an airline ticket purchase, where the customer takes pot luck on availability. With these kinds of arrangement, salons are still generating business and maximising on the most profitable use of their staff time. While they are mindful of their reputation for style and customer satisfaction, you maintain your right as a customer to be choosy. Such arrangements are of mutual convenience.

Where to seek objective advice

Women who seek a re-assessment of their hair are often at a loss as to where to go for objective advice. What effect will a perm achieve? Will it damage their hair? How long will it last? Should they leave their hair to grey naturally or should they have it coloured? What are the options open to them? How long will treatments last? How much are they likely to cost?

The dilemma is this. How can anyone expect busy hairdressers to give a considered, unbiased opinion when they have a vested interest in selling the most expensive treatment? The fact that so many women suffer from over-processed hair is not reassuring.

One possible solution is to make a separate appointment for a consultation first before making the decision about a treatment. Perhaps a better possibility is to seek advice through a college or training centre. Brian Bates, from the Incorporated Guild of Hairdressers, Wigmakers and Perfumers, believes that 'people in a teaching or training environment are making every effort to please and you will certainly get a fair assessment there'. However, he does give the warning that before attending as a model for teaching purposes, you should make sure that the establishment, be it a college or private school, is an accredited training centre taking City and Guilds examinations.

Going as a model

Hairdressers require models for practice at various stages of their training, which is usually a three-year apprenticeship. Even qualified hairdressers continue to attend courses to update their knowledge of new products and techniques, particularly where colouring is concerned.

Whenever a salon places an advertisement in its window for models, it usually states what is on offer and at what price. Colleges which run hairdressing courses don't necessarily advertise; they usually find willing participants by word of mouth. If there is a college near you which runs a hairdressing course, you can make enquiries about models by telephoning the course tutor. Check the fee, which is usually nominal. If you are nervous about absolute beginners, ask what stage the students have reached. Remember, they will be always be supervised.

The advantages of going as a model are set out below:

There is a big saving in price, especially for otherwise expensive treatments such as perms and colouring.

You will have the reassurance that these processes will be performed in a teaching atmosphere, where the hairdresser is not distracted by other clients.

At a college, you will also enjoy an unbiased assessment on the condition of your hair and useful advice about how to handle it.

There are three disadvantages.

Sessions usually take longer; you need to allow for a student working more slowly than an experienced stylist, and for consultation times with the supervisor.

Appointments will be limited to certain times and days; perhaps only evenings in the case of a salon.

Colleges tend to shut down regularly for lengthy holidays.

Mobile hairdressers

There are many hairdressers who will do your hair in your own home by appointment and bring their own equipment. They usually advertise their services in the local press, and their prices compare favourably with local salons.

This service has obvious advantages if you are not very mobile and find it difficult to get to a salon, or if you have arthritis or stiffness in your shoulders and find hair care difficult or painful. However, there are other benefits too.

A home hairdresser may be available in the evenings or at other times when salons are closed. This may be particularly useful for special occasion hairdressing when you may want to wear a hair ornament such as a velvet bow, or a hairpiece.

The home hairdresser can cut hair for more than one member of the family on the same visit. This may be the perfect opportunity to persuade your partner to forsake the hairstyle of a lifetime.

Men, in particular, may like to have the benefit of professional colouring in the privacy of their own home.

Having a perm in the comfort of your own home is more pleasant and saves time. You have the hairdresser's full attention and won't be 'over-permed'.

Clearly it is important to know whether or not a home hairdresser is properly qualified. He or she should be able to produce an indemnity certificate or public liability policy showing that he or she carries appropriate insurance. This protects both parties since it enables the customer to claim compensation should there be a need to pay for remedial treatment, and it permits the hairdresser to claim compensation in case of damage to their equipment due to the customer's faulty electrical wiring.

Hairstyles for thinning hair

The kind of hair you possess, curly or straight, fine or coarse, thick or thin, is based on genetic inheritance. People learn from experience that it's sensible to match your style to your hair-type. This is commonsense at any age.

The ageing process does, however, create additional limitations in style. Men have to cope with a receding hair-line and thinning on the crown – male pattern baldness, as it is known. Women may experience overall thinning. These changes occur over a period of time; how quickly they take place and at what age depends on the individual, with family patterns again playing a major part.

The best advice for men is to be positive, not negative, about baldness. Work with it, not against it.

If your hair is thinning, keep it short and well cut to the shape of the head.

Avoid long strands of hair which only accentuate sparseness elsewhere.

Resist very low partings in an effort to distribute the hair more thickly; they are a give-away.

Don't comb long strands over a bald patch. Not only is it not an effective disguise, it positively draws attention to the baldness and has become a subject for comedy.

Facial hair can compensate. You may wish to consider growing a beard or moustache.

Women with thinning hair may find the following guidelines helpful. Again, be positive.

A straight style may no longer be the most flattering.

Solutions to disguise thinning include a soft perm, regular salon visits, the frequent use of conditioner to give body, as well as products such as mousse. Beware of using too much mousse at one time since it can weigh the hair down.

Consider all-one-length cutting, like a bob, rather than layered cutting which thins the hair out.

Extra fullness can be achieved by bending forward when you dry the hair, with the head held downwards. You can either dry your hair with a blow dryer or naturally, by running your fingers through the hair.

Another way to create the illusion of additional body is by parting the hair in lined sections, using hairspray along the hairlines and then allowing it to dry. Don't overdo this: overuse of hairspray can cause a residue resulting in dandruff.

Older women should be wary of generalisations, however. There are always exceptions to the average and decisions should be based on individual circumstances. Just as the choice of clothes depends not on age but on body shape, so a hairstyle depends more on the condition of the hair. Some older women with strong bone structures look very attractive with a close-cut crop, the grey or silver making a wonderful foil for dramatic earrings.

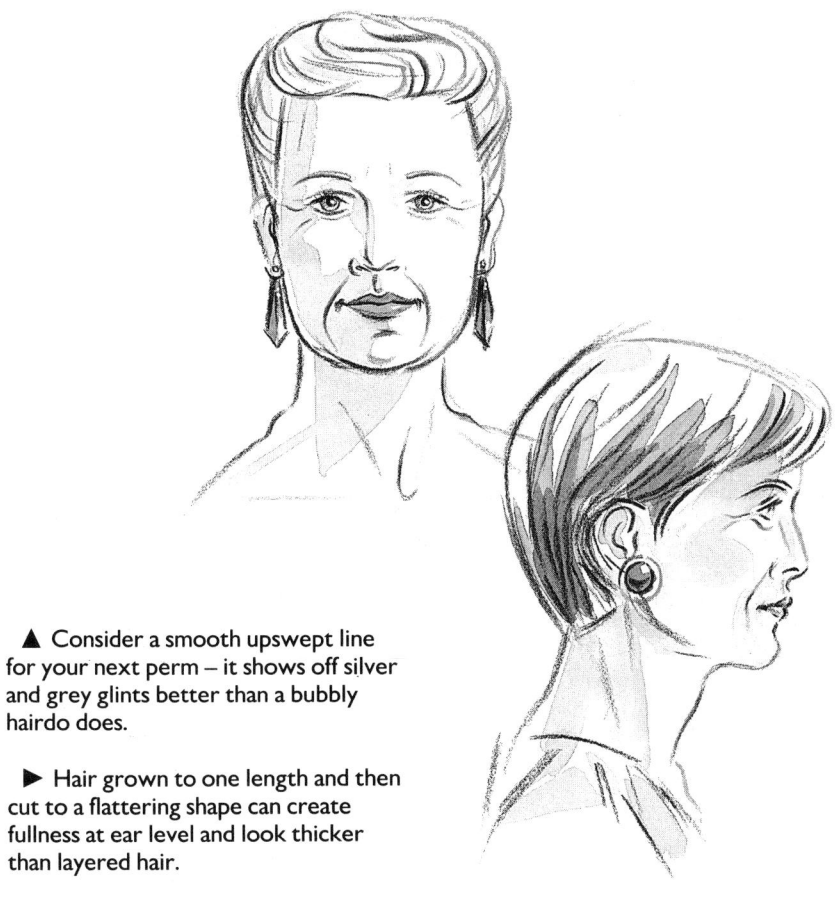

▲ Consider a smooth upswept line for your next perm – it shows off silver and grey glints better than a bubbly hairdo does.

▶ Hair grown to one length and then cut to a flattering shape can create fullness at ear level and look thicker than layered hair.

Hair loss

Hair is constantly being shed at an average rate of 20–80 hairs per day throughout our lives. Some people even notice an autumn or spring moult when they are conscious of more hairs than usual blocking the plughole after shampooing. There is no special treatment for hair thinning, other than normal care. What you can do is adapt your hairstyle accordingly. Creative solutions could include the use of cotton or silk scarves or an embroidered or beaded cap.

Male pattern baldness, which starts with a receding hair-line and thinning on the crown, is also part of the natural process of ageing. The average rate of hair loss is reckoned at 40 per cent at age 40, 50 per cent at age 50 and 60 per cent at age 60. Men should be especially wary of advertisements with exaggerated claims to treat or cure baldness. This doesn't mean that you should reject out of hand the many and varied forms of hair replacement. You should, however, seek impartial advice first. Accurate diagnosis, classification of the type and cause of hair loss and suitability of the individual for any particular treatment are vital factors.

The Institute of Trichologists (see p 145) have their own Scalp and Hair Hospital in South London. This is run as a registered charity and outpatient appointments are available at subsidised rates. The Institute can also supply information by post including a countrywide list of registered member trichologists. Information about sudden hair loss can be found on page 140.

Wigs, toupées and hair pieces

Wigs

A wig can be a major asset, a necessary prop following hair loss through chemotherapy, neurosurgery and other causes.

A wig or hairpiece can be a real life enhancer, as many older women with thinning or wispy fine hair have discovered. They know from experience the difference a wig can make to their total appearance, and that a permanently well-styled hairdo sets off their clothes. Some women possess two or three wigs in different styles or for different purposes. Others prefer to supplement existing hair with a matching hairpiece, such as a chignon.

Men, too, can drastically change their appearance by wearing a hairpiece or toupée (see sketches on p 132). While it is all very well for outsiders to pronounce that baldness is not unattractive and to cite Telly Savalas and Yul Brynner as examples of attractive bald men, it is your confidence and self-esteem which are at stake. However, you need to consider carefully whether you will be able to carry off the deception involved in wearing a toupée. It quite often happens that a man will buy one but then can't bring himself to wear it.

Where do you buy a wig?

Anyone entitled to an NHS-prescribed wig will automatically be put in touch with whichever wig specialist in the area holds the NHS contract. This firm will probably order its wigs from one of the major suppliers such as Banbury Postiche (see p 143), which also deals direct with the public. Another major supplier is Floridan (see p 145) which, as well as supplying wig specialists, also has its own outlets in 50 or so leading department stores.

Wig-making: an expensive craft

Wigs and hairpieces do not damage the scalp or the natural hair since today's products are lightweight and have mesh linings to allow for easy air circulation. A typical woman's wig uses some 50,000 hairs, all knotted to a carefully selected foundation. It takes six months to learn just one type of knotting, and there are several. Much of the expertise in wig-making depends on selecting the foundation material, the type of gauze or net which will mould best to the shape of the head and give the greatest comfort. Male toupées need a special lining because of a problem with static electricity from the client's existing hair. Creating natural-looking partings calls for particular skill.

In view of the work involved, it comes as no surprise that an exclusively handcrafted hairpiece, made from carefully matched hair, is costly. The expense does not end there either. The human hair used in wigs has been previously bleached and dyed. In time it will fade and require specialised cleaning and redressing, a maintenance service which a major supplier like Banbury provides.

As well as made-to-measure wigs and hairpieces, Banbury also stocks a wide range of acrylic fibre wigs and hairpieces, in every size and many colours, including a range of greys and whites. The main advantage with a synthetic product is that it is cheaper, lighter and easier to look after at home.

Buying and maintaining a wig

To find out more about which wig or hairpiece is right for you, you can make an appointment with a consultant. Such consultants will always advise you to buy a good ready-made acrylic piece if they believe it will suit your lifestyle.

Floridan concentrates on ready-made synthetic ladies' wigs and ready-made toupées. The women's range is marketed under the name Ginchy; the men's range is called Olympus. Many of the wig and toupée specialists supplied by Floridan provide a mail order service; some will visit housebound clients in their own home for a small additional fee.

The following tips will help you to get the best out of a wig.

- **P**ut your wig on front first, like a bathing cap. Comb out a few strands of your own hair from the front and sides and mix them in to create a soft natural hairline.
- **A**lways wash your synthetic wig in cool water using a special wig shampoo. Rinse the wig well, using a drop of fabric conditioner in the water. Shake the wig out and leave it to dry overnight on a door knob or collapsible wig stand.

◀ A wig or hairpiece can be a real life-enhancer, so long as it feels comfortable and looks natural. This toupée is by Floridan and available through wig specialists.

SPECIAL NEEDS

NO ONE IN THE WORLD CAN MAKE YOU FEEL INFERIOR WITHOUT YOUR CONSENT

Eleanor Roosevelt

■

Ageing is a process we all share and experience and to which we must adapt. In addition to the natural process, however, many people must adapt to a changed body which may not look or function as it once used to. Looking attractive matters even more: your spirits need more of a lift. Knowing that you are looking your best can make a considerable difference to how you face each day.

Special problems need special solutions. Fortunately there are support groups as well as voluntary organisations who can help with practical information and advice about all aspects of your appearance.

Keeping in touch with the latest developments may offer solutions to old problems. Technology is continually discovering and updating materials which can greatly improve the performance and appearance of existing products. Many artificial, clumsy and inelegant items are being replaced by more efficient and acceptable designs. Typical examples of recently improved products are easy-care, natural-looking wigs for those with hair loss; lightweight and washable replacement breast forms to slip inside a bra after breast surgery; less bulky, better fitting, leakproof pads and pants for those with bladder problems; skin camouflage creams for men and women with birth marks and other skin blemishes.

For most problems affecting the appearance, there is a solution available. You may have to search and experiment to find the most appropriate product for your individual needs, but help is invariably there once you decide to look for it.

After breast surgery

Many women every year have to go into hospital to have a breast removed; counselling on how to cope both emotionally and practically after such surgery should start immediately after the operation. Many hospitals nowadays have Breast Care Nurses, sometimes called Mastectomy Nurses, who offer advice and support.

The Breast Care and Mastectomy Association of Great Britain (see p 143) has compiled a leaflet *Exercises after breast surgery* to help you regain the full range of arm movements. BCMA's booklet *Looking good after breast surgery* gives information, not only about prostheses (breast forms), but about choosing bras, beachwear, pretty nightwear and low-cut evening dresses. A video showing how other women have coped is also available.

You may of course have had your mastectomy some years ago when information about clothes and appearance wasn't so readily available. There are now many kinds of prosthesis available, including BCMA's own 'Cumfie'. At its premises you can actually try on a range of bras and swimwear which you can then order direct from their list of stockists. This service is being continually updated.

Radiotherapy sometimes leaves blemish marks on the skin and these can be concealed with cover camouflage creams. The BCMA stocklist gives details of manufacturers. It may be possible for you to obtain these on prescription from your GP.

Bent backs and height loss

Osteoporosis, the bone density disease which affects one in four older women, can result in a curving of the spine, a loss of height, a shortened chest cavity and a tummy bulge. Off-the-peg clothes no longer fit; necklines gape at the back; tops are too tight under the arms; skirts and trousers come right up under the bust.

A couple of years ago the National Osteoporosis Society (NOS) approached the London College of Fashion. Twelve female osteoporosis sufferers teamed up with final-year BTech/HND students, who undertook a special project designing individual outfits to disguise their clients' weak points. The resulting colourful and glamorous creations were modelled by the women at a fashion show, compèred by NOS patron Lizzie Webb, well-known to *TV-AM* exercise watchers.

It proved neither practical nor possible to produce a range of patterns to suit all osteoporosis sufferers since physical characteristics are individual. What did emerge from the project, however, was an inspiring booklet *Straighten up with fashion,* full of ideas for flattering styles and ways to disguise the most common problems, together with suggested simple alterations to off-the-peg garments. The booklet is obtainable from the Society at the address on page 146.

Dressing difficulties

Comfortable, washable and attractive clothes in roomy styles which are easy to get in and out of, and with the minimum of awkward fastenings, are hard to find in the shops. Yet anyone whose shoulders are stiff with arthritis knows what an enormous difference these features make to getting dressed in the morning, particularly if you live alone.

The Special Collection is the name of a mail order catalogue from the established Manchester firm of J D Williams (see p 146). The collection includes clothes for men and women; not only daywear but nightwear, underwear and shoes in five widths. What makes the collection special, besides the elasticated waists and the step-in styles, is the size range: women's sizes range from 10–30; for men, chest sizes range from 34" – 58". The garments are designed with wheelchair-users in mind so that they won't bunch or ride up.

The catalogue was compiled with the help of the Disabled Living Foundation (see p 145). This organisation runs its own clothing and footwear advisory service to assist members of the public who have disability problems, especially those who use wheelchairs and those who wear special pants and pads because of incontinence. In addition, there are 30 Disabled Living Centres throughout the country where clothing and equipment is displayed and where individual advice can be obtained by prior appointment. If there is a Centre near you, it will be listed in the telephone directory; otherwise write for the countrywide list to the address on page 144.

Help with continence

Leaking or dribbling is a miserable embarrassment which ruins the lives of many people, making them unnecessarily housebound. It is not a normal part of ageing and the causes are many and varied. The condition can often be treated, or at least coped with successfully so that you can lead a normal social life. Special pads, pants and devices are available from many specialist suppliers. Initial sources of advice are your GP, district nurse or health visitor who will know if there is a local continence advisor – a specially-trained nurse well used to problem solving. In the first instance, it is vital to seek the right source of advice.

A free fact sheet *Help with Incontinence* is available from Age Concern England. Please enclose a 9" x 6" stamped, self-addressed envelope. Age Concern's publication *In Control – Help with Incontinence* is also full of helpful information.

Allergies

Choosing an appropriate branded product is the right of every consumer. Cosmetic ingredient labelling has been mandatory in the United States since 1977, but this right is denied to people in the UK. We don't even have a 'flash warning' system of labelling which would go some way to alert high-risk consumers, like the three million people in the UK who suffer from eczema, and who are concerned about safe products.

Rights and risks

The laxity in product labelling adversely affects us all. Each one of us is a cosmetics consumer, whether we like it or not. Included within the definition of cosmetic products are creams, soaps, shampoos, toothpastes and deodorants, quite apart from colour cosmetics and hair colourants.

An individual may develop an allergy to a cosmetic ingredient at any time in his or her life. Playing safe and trying to avoid potential risks is not just a matter of refusing to buy unnecessary products, like purple eyeshadow or highly perfumed preparations. Many of the problem ingredients are present in all products – even the most basic.

Since an allergic reaction may not develop until 48–72 hours after exposure to the skin, it isn't always obvious to the users, or their doctors, what the cause has been. Doctors at skin clinics can waste hours of NHS time searching for unidentified irritants. Yet even when the substance causing the reaction has been identified and the condition treated, the individual has no means of avoiding it in future purchases. He or she may stop buying the specific product which triggered the reaction, but the substance itself may well be used in other preparations. Without any indication on the packaging, there is no means of knowing. It is particularly galling that major European manufacturers selling to the North American market comply with the regulations in force in the USA while their European customers get no protection whatsoever.

The British Association of Dermatologists, a professional body of medical skin specialists, which is concerned and alarmed at the million or more patients in the UK who suffer from adverse reactions, has launched a public awareness campaign. Its aim is to bring about the introduction of an article requiring full ingredient labelling into European legislation and thereby provide a measure of protection for those who suffer allergic reactions.

A special service

Almay is well known as a leading skincare company whose fragrance-free products are formulated and manufactured to reduce allergic reaction to a minimum. While irritation or sensitisation seldom arise from the use of an Almay product, there is the occasional patient who may be allergic to the small concentration of parabens, the main preservative in Almay cosmetics. Wherever feasible, individual formulations eliminating offending ingredients can be provided by Almay at nominal cost. For further information, contact Almay Cosmetics (see p 143).

Skin blemishes

Skin camouflage creams can be used by men and women to cover a wide range of skin conditions, including birthmarks and port wine stains.

Vitiligo is a skin condition which results in pure white patches appearing on the skin. Although it can affect anyone of any race, regardless of skin colour, it is particularly distressing for people with dark skins. One company, D.D.C (London) Ltd (see p 144), manufacturers of Dermablend Corrective Cosmetics, also keeps the Flori Roberts range, specially formulated for black skins. It also runs a beauty salon on its premises in Notting Hill Gate which offers free advice. There is also a Vitiligo Support Group (see p 146).

Sometimes camouflage creams are available on prescription from your GP if recommended by a skin camouflage therapist. Additional help with camouflage is also available from the British Red Cross; contact your local branch for further information or write to the London address on page 144.

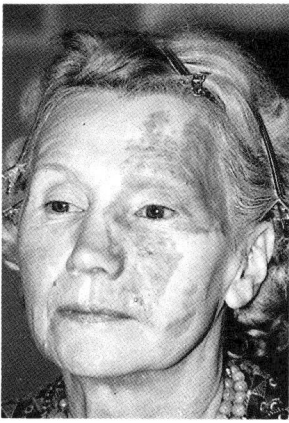

◀ Help with camouflage of skin problems is available from the British Red Cross, as is guidance in making-up for the visually impaired.

Stockists of camouflage creams include the Yorkshire firm Thomas Blake & Co, which makes a product called Veil Cover Cream; samples by post from the address on page 146.

Make-up lessons for the partially sighted

The British Red Cross has played a big part in pioneering the use of volunteers to teach blind and partially-sighted women to apply make-up. Enquire first at your local branch before contacting the London office (see p 144).

More recently, Body Shop has been training some of their staff to advise partially-sighted customers. They have also produced a helpful cassette.

Overweight and housebound?

For those unable to attend a group run by Weight Watchers for whatever reason, the company offers a postal service using a system of progress cards and telephone counselling by trained lecturers who have already helped many people lose weight successfully. Members can enrol for a minimum of six weeks at a time.

Hair

Sudden hair loss

Sudden hair loss can happen at any age. Sometimes the condition needs medical investigation, as when sudden shock or stress acts as a trigger and upsets the natural hormone balance of the body. Occasionally, there may be a thyroid deficiency, an allergy or a scalp disorder. Sometimes the hair loss is a side-effect, caused by medical treatment of another condition; chemotherapy is the most common example of this, but certain anti-gout, anti-arthritis and anti-depressant drugs can also affect some patients this way.

Whatever the reason, the effects of sudden hair loss are distressing for the sufferer. In addition to medical advice, patients can also get support from a self-help group called Hairline International (see p 145). This group was started by a writer and broadcaster, Elizabeth Steel, whose own hair loss was caused through the scalp disease alopecia areata. As a result of her traumatic experience, she wrote a book – *Coping with Sudden Hair Loss* (see p 147).

Hair replacement

There are many different methods and techniques of hair replacement. Not all of them are suitable for everyone, and each has its limitations. Impartial advice based on a personal consultation should be obtained from a qualified trichologist.

Non-surgical methods of hair replacement include hair bonding and weaving; another method involves a toupée postiche (a wig) being permanently attached to the scalp by tunnel grafts.

Punch grafting is a surgical technique of hair transplantation, and is the form of cosmetic surgery most frequently performed in the world. However, it is only possible provided the patient's own donor zone of existing hair is of sufficient density in proportion to the bald area. The operation must be performed by a qualified surgeon.

A widely publicised drug treatment for hair replacement, Minoxidil therapy, can only be prescribed by a doctor because of its side-effects on blood pressure. The same drug in a more concentrated form is used to lower blood pressure, which is how its hair-growing possibilities came to be discovered. The brand name of Minoxidil is Regaine. It is not available on the NHS, is expensive, involves external application twice a day and has enjoyed only modest success. Advanced cases of baldness of long duration have little or no chance of benefitting from its use. It seems to be more effective when only small areas of hair growth are involved, and even then regrowth is claimed to be fuzzy. Its American manufacturers may find that the female market for the product is potentially greater than the male.

In spite of its present limitations, Minoxidil has proved to be the most promising breakthrough to date in the age-old search for a cure for baldness. Scientists are working in the area of drug treatment expect more hopeful results in about five years.

No Spring nor Summer
beauty hath such grace
As I have seen in one
Autumnal face
■

JOHN DONNE

Further Information

Useful addresses

Academy of Colour and Style
6 Dingle Dell
Leighton Buzzard
Bedfordshire LU7 7JL
Tel: 0525 375041

Acorn Designs
Fala House, Fala
Pathhead
Midlothian EH37 5SY
Tel: 087 533 679

Advertising Standards Authority
Brook House
2-16 Torrington Place
London WC1E 7HN
Tel: 071-580 5555

Alcohol Concern
305 Gray's Inn Road
London WC1X 8QS

Almay Cosmetics
Nicholas Laboratories
225 Bath Road, Slough
Berkshire SL1 4AU
Tel: 0753 523971

Avon Cosmetics Ltd
Nunn Mills Road
Northampton NN1 5PA
Tel: 0604 232425

Banbury Postiche
Little Bourton House
Southam Road, Banbury
Oxon OX16 7SR
Tel: 0295 750606

Breast Care and Mastectomy Association of Great Britain
15–19 Britten Street
London SW3 3TZ
Tel: 071–867 1103 (help line)
071-867 8275 (administration line)
and

9 Castle Terrace
Edinburgh EH1 2DP
Tel: 031–228 6715

British Association of International Beauty Therapy and Cosmetology Ltd
2nd Floor
34 Imperial Square
Cheltenham
Gloucestershire GL50 1QZ
Tel: 0242 570284

British Dental Association
64 Wimpole Street
London W1M 8AL
Tel: 071–935 0875

British Dental Health Foundation
Eastlands Court
St Peter's Road, Rugby
Warwickshire CV21 3QP
Tel: 0788 546365

British Footwear Manufacturers Federation
Royalty House
72 Dean Street
London W1V 5HB
Tel: 071–437 5573

British Red Cross
9 Grosvenor Crescent
London SW1X 7EJ
Tel: 071–235 5454

British Wheel of Yoga
1 Hamilton Place
Boston Road
Sleaford NG34 7ES
Tel: 0529 306851

Button Box
44 Bedford Street
Covent Garden
London WC2E 9HA
Tel: 071–240 2716

Button Queen
19 Marylebone Lane
London W1M 5FE
Tel: 071-935 1505

Colour Me Beautiful
66 Abbey Business Centre
Ingate Place
London SW8 3NS
Tel: 071–627 5211

Colourflair
188 Warren Road
Woodingdean
Brighton BN2 6DD
Tel: 0273 6505540

Cosmetics to Go
29 High Street
Poole
Dorset BH15 1AB
Tel: 0800 373 366 (free)

Crafts Council
44A Pentonville Road
London N1 9BY
Tel: 071–278 7700

D.D.C (London) Ltd
158 Notting Hill Gate
London W11 3GQ
Tel: 071–229 4224

Disabled Living Centres Council
380-384 Harrow Road
London W9 2HU
Tel: 071–266 2059

Disabled Living Foundation
380–384 Harrow Road
London W9 2HU
Tel: 071–289 6111

EXTEND
1A North Street
Sheringham
Norfolk NR26 8LJ
Tel: 0263 822479

First Impressions
Downing Park
Swaffham Bulbeck
Cambridge CB5 0NW
Tel: 0223 813121

Floridan Group Limited
Parkside Avenue
Two Station Lane
Witney
Oxon OX8 6YF
Tel: 0993 702992

Hairline International
39 St Johns Close
Knowle
Solihull
West Midlands B93 0NN

High & Mighty
The Old School House
High Street
Hungerford
Berkshire RG17 0NF
Tel: 0488 684666

House of Colour
4 Dudrich House
Princes Lane
London N10 3LU
Tel: 081–444 3621

Inglewood Health Hydro
Templeton Road
Kintbury
Nr Newbury
Berkshire RG15 0SW
Tel: 0488 682022

Institute of Clinical Aromatherapy
22 Bromley Road
London SE6 2TP
Tel: 081–690 6681

Institute of Complementary Medicine
3 Cochrane House
Admirals Way
London E14
Tel: 0839 300 601 (Information line)

Institute of Trichologists
228 Stockwell Road
London SW9 9SU
Tel: 071–733 2056

Jafra Cosmetics International
2 Eelmoor Road
Farnborough
Hampshire GU14 7QN
Tel: 0252 517474

Jean Guthrie Beauty Care
2 Lamont Road
London SW10 0HL
Tel: 071–352 4809

James Meade Limited
48 Charlton Road
Andover
Hampshire SP10 3JL
Tel: 0264 333 222

Joan Price's Face Place
33 Cadogan Street
Chelsea
London SW3 2PP
Tel: 071–589 9062

Liv-in-Leather (Wakefield) Ltd
61 Northgate
Wakefield
W Yorkshire WF1 3BP
Tel: 0924 371288

Long Tall Sally
3 Quarry Park Close
Moulton Park
Northanpton NN3 1QB
Tel: 0604 494349

Martha Hill
FREEPOST
The Old Vicarage
Laxton
Northamptonshire NN17 3BR
Tel: 078 085 259

National Osteoporosis Society
PO Box 10
Radstock
Bath BA3 3YB
Tel: 0761 32472

National Society of Non-Smokers (QUIT)
102 Gloucester Place
London W1H 3DA
Tel: 071-487 3000

One of Gillies
Llantrithyd
Cowbridge, S Glamorgan
Wales CF7 7UB
Tel: 0446 781357

Patra Selections
1-5 Nant Road
London NW2 2AL
Tel: 081-209 1112

SFL (Special Offers)
Charnham Lane
Hungerford
Berkshire RG17 0QQ
Tel: 0488 682020

Society of Shoe Fitters
The Anchorage
28 Admiral's Walk
Hingham, Norfolk NR9 4JL

Thomas Blake & Co
The Byre House
Fearby, Nr Masham
North Yorkshire HG4 4NF
Tel: 0765 689042

Vitiligo Group
PO Box 919
London SE21 8AW
Tel: 081-776 7022

Weight Watchers (UK) Ltd
Kidwells Park House
Kidwells Park Drive
Maidenhead
Berkshire SL6 8YT
Tel: 0628 777077

J D Williams
PO Box 285
53 Dale Street
Manchester M60 6ES

Wool Works
48 Friar Street
Worcester WR1 2NA
Tel: 0905 29228

Your True Colours
Studio 8
50 Belsize Square
London NW3 4HN
Tel: 071-435 0726

Yoga for Health Foundation
Ickwell Bury
Biggleswade
Bedfordshire SG18 9EF
Tel: 076727 271

Recommended reading

Always in Style, Pooser, Doris, £7.95. (Piatkus, 1987).

Archer's Good Clothes Guide, £5.99. (Ebury Press). An annual publication.

Colour for Men, Jackson, Carole, with Lulow, Kalia, £6.95. (Piatkus, 1984).

Colour Me Beautiful, Jackson, Carole, £6.95. (Piatkus, 1983).

Coping with Sudden Hair Loss, Steel, Elizabeth, £5.99 (Thorsons, 1988).

Eva Fraser's Facial Workout, Fraser, Eva, £8.99 (Viking, 1991). An accompanying video is available from Virgin Records.

Factory Shop Guides, Cutress, Gillian (ed). Gillian Cutress, 34 Park Hill, London SW4 9PB (tel: 071–622 3722). Regional editions, updated annually.

Look Ten Years Younger, Feel Ten Years Better, Scala, Dr James, and Jacques, Barbara, £12.95. (Piatkus, 1991).

The Colour and Style File, Jacques, Barbara, £10.95 (Piatkus, 1989).

The Complete Style Guide from Colour Me Beautiful, Spillane, Mary, £14.95. (Piatkus, 1991).

About Age Concern

Looking Good, Feeling Good, is one of a wide range of titles published by Age Concern England – the National Council on Ageing. In addition, Age Concern England is actively engaged in training, information provision, research and campaigning for retired people and those who work with them. It is a registered charity dependent on public support for the continuation of its work.

Age Concern England links closely with Age Concern centres in Scotland, Wales and Northern Ireland to form a network of over 1,400 independent local UK groups. These groups, with the invaluable help of an estimated 250,000 volunteers, aim to improve the quality of life for older people and develop services appropriate to local needs and resources. These include advice and information, day care, visiting services, transport schemes, clubs and specialist facilities for physically and mentally frail older people.

Age Concern England
1268 London Road
London SW16 4ER
Tel: 081-679 8000

Age Concern Scotland
54a Fountainbridge
Edinburgh EH3 9PT
Tel: 031-228 5656

Age Concern Wales
4th Floor
1 Cathedral Road
Cardiff CF1 9SD
Tel: 0222 371821/371566

Age Concern Northern Ireland
6 Lower Crescent
Belfast BT7 1NR
Tel: 0232 245729

Publications from ACE Books

A wide range of titles is published by Age Concern England under the ACE Books imprint.

Money matters

Using Your Home as Capital
Cecil Hinton

This best-selling book for home-owners, which is updated annually, gives a detailed explanation of how to capitalise on the value of your home and obtain a regular additional income.

Price on application

Your Taxes and Savings
Sally West and Jennie Hawthorne

The complexities of our tax system as they affect older people and the investment opportunities open to them are explained in straightforward terms in this valuable annual guide.

Price on application

Your Rights
Sally West

A highly acclaimed annual guide to State benefits available to older people. Contains current information on Income Support, Housing Benefit and Retirement Pensions among other matters and provides advice on how to claim them.

Price on application

General

Living, Loving and Ageing: Sexual and personal relationships in later life
Wendy Greengross and Sally Greengross

Sexuality is often regarded as the preserve of the younger generation. At last, here is a book for older people, and those who work with them,

which tackles the issues in a straightforward fashion, avoiding preconceptions and bias.
£4.95 0–86242–070–9

Life in the Sun: A guide to long-stay holidays and living abroad in retirement
Nancy Tuft
Every year millions of older people consider either taking long-stay holidays or moving abroad on a more permanent basis. This essential guide examines the pitfalls associated with such a move and tackles topics varying from pets to packing.
£6.95 0–86242–085–7

Out and About: A travel and transport guide
Richard Armitage and John Taylor
A comprehensive source of information on travel and transport for older people and others with limited mobility. Whether planning a trip to the local shops or a journey abroad, this book provides a step-by-step guide to the arrangements that need to be made. As well as general information, there is a detailed section on the modes of transport available and a list of addresses for further help and advice.
£6.95 0–86242–092-X

Housing

A Buyer's Guide to Sheltered Housing
Age Concern England and the NHTPC
Buying a flat or bungalow in a sheltered scheme? This guide provides vital information on the running costs, design and management of schemes to help you make an informed decision.
£2.50 0–86242–063–6

An Owner's Guide: Your Home in Retirement
Age Concern England and the NHTPC
A guide to ways in which older owner-occupiers can make their homes more comfortable and easier to manage. Advice is given on topics such as repairs and maintenance, heating, insulation and home security.

There is also information on adapting a home for disabled residents and the sort of grants available for such work.
£2.50 0-86242-095-4

Housing Options for Older People
David Bookbinder
A review of housing options is part of growing older. All the possibilities and their practical implications are carefully considered in this comprehensive guide.
Price on application

Health

The Foot Care Book: An A-Z of fitter feet
Judith Kemp SRCh
A self-help guide for elderly people on routine foot care, this book includes an A-Z of problems and a guide to who's who in foot care.
£2.95 0-86242-066-0

Your Health in Retirement
Dr J A Muir Gray and Pat Blair
This book is a comprehensive source of information to help readers look after themselves and work towards better health. Produced in an accessible A-Z style, full details are given of people and useful organisations from which assistance can be sought.
£4.50 0-86242-082-2

If you would like to order any of these titles, please write to the address below, enclosing a cheque or money order for the appropriate amount. A complete list of publications is available on request.
Credit card orders may be made on 081-679 8000.
Age Concern England (DEPT LG1)
1268 London Road
FREEPOST
London SW16 4ER

Information Factsheets

Age Concern England produces over 30 factsheets on a variety of subjects. Single copies are free on receipt of a 9" x 6" sae. If you require a selection of factsheets or multiple copies, charges will be given on request.

A complete set of factsheets is available in a ring binder at the current cost of £30, which includes the first year's subscription. The current cost for annual subscription for subsequent years is £12. There are different rates of subscription for people living abroad.

Factsheets are revised and updated throughout the year and membership of the subscription service will ensure that your information is always current.

Write to the Information and Policy Department at the address given on page 151 for further information.